Winning Local Elections

A GUIDE TO WINNING ELECTIONS AT THE LOCAL AND STATE LEGISLATIVE LEVELS

Daniel O'Connell Theno

Copyright © 2018 Daniel O'Connell Theno
First Edition

All rights reserved.
ISBN-13: 9781726023306

To my family and supporters who were always there with me going door-to-door, assembling signs, handing out buttons, smiling and waving through countless parades, and stuffing thousands of envelopes.

Thank you.

Table of Contents

Table of Contents i
About This Book iii
Takeaways v
Chapter 1: Getting Started 1
Chapter 2: The Campaign Organization 21
Chapter 3: Budget and Finance 37
Chapter 4: Media Relations and Free Publicity 53
Chapter 5: General Principles of Campaign Advertising ... 69
Chapter 6: Media Advertising Budgets and Ad Types 87
Chapter 7: Print Media Advertising 101
Chapter 8: Electronic Media Advertising 119
Chapter 9: Campaign Materials and Mailings 141
Chapter 10: Events and Appearances 161
Chapter 11: Going After the Opponent 179
Chapter 12: Getting Ready For the Next Campaign 193

About This Book

Many people want to run for public office but they just don't know how to get started or how to run an effective campaign to get elected. A person declaring his or her candidacy is one thing. Unless that declaration is followed up by a campaign that convinces voters that the person is the best choice for office, it means nothing.

I was helping a friend win a seat in the Ohio Legislature and halfway through the campaign he said "Dan, you really know a lot about how to organize and run a campaign. You really should write a book to help others who are seeking public office." When I retired I made this book a top priority.

This book isn't for someone running for President, Governor or the United States Senate. People running for those offices have consultants and advisors and their campaigns rely heavily on TV advertising. This book is for the amateur who wants to run for a local, county, school district or state legislative office and needs to organize and execute a winning campaign. Other people who have already run a few campaigns may have the same advice to share. Then again, even an experienced elected official may find some pages of this book new and innovative.

This book contains a banquet of ideas and suggestions that a candidate can pick and choose from to suit to his or her campaign. The character of each campaign is different and depends on the candidate, the issues that resonate with voters and the nature of the community or district where the campaign is being conducted. Ordering yard signs for a downtown Los Angeles state legislative seat probably isn't a wise investment. Going door-to-door in a rural Montana district might not be practical. As you read through this book jot down tips that are relevant to your campaign. Having said that, there are some things I am advising all candidates NOT to do which apply to all campaigns.

Friends who proofed this book found it easy to read, fun and informative. I hope you will feel the same way.

Takeaways

Whenever you see a shaded box, it's a "Takeaway". If you remember nothing else from each section, keep these tidbits of wisdom in mind. Hopefully they will remind you of important things to consider for you to be successful.

Chapter 1: Getting Started

You have decided that you would like to run for political office. You have taken a good step to success by reading this book. In this chapter we will examine some of the initial thought processes and communications you should initiate in the early phases of your campaign.

Why are you running?

There are many reasons why people run for political office. Most often it's because they have an interest in government and believe their contributions can have a positive impact on policy development. Some people become candidates because others have encouraged them to do so. Some people run for office to prevent someone they distrust or dislike form getting elected. There are even candidates who run with the expectation or hope that they will *lose*. They may be just getting their names known for when an incumbent is expected to retire or to fill the ticket for a political party.

So, what is your reason for running? The best reason for running is that you feel you can win and that your service will be beneficial to your community, state or nation. You should thoroughly examine your reason for running because that will determine how your campaign is organized and executed. For purposes of this guide, we will assume that your intentions are totally altruistic and that you really want to *win*.

> **The best reason for running is that you feel that you can win and that your service will be beneficial to your community, state or nation.**

Do you have confidence?

Are you an introvert or an extrovert? There is a term for a candidate who is shy, laid-back, and lacks self-esteem. It's called "defeated candidate". You have to be somewhat of an egomaniac to run for political office. You will be spending a lot of time selling yourself and your ideas to complete strangers. If you are not confident about yourself, your abilities to campaign, win an election and govern effectively, political office is not for you.

> **Introverts seldom make good candidates. A candidate has to have an ego without being egotistical.**

What is your platform?

I contend that the intelligence, appearance, and likability of a candidate are usually more important than the issues of a campaign. However, a candidate must have some issues and reasons why he or she is running in order to get elected.

Whatever issues a candidate states he or she will work for if elected, there are three rules in presenting those issues to the public... Rule #1: Issues should be stated in a clear, but brief manner. One line or one sentence is often enough. Rule #2: The list of major issues should be short. Three to five issues in most campaigns is plenty. Rule #3: If a candidate doesn't follow Rule #1 and Rule #2 a candidate is going to have a tough time getting elected.

A candidate would be wise to run issues past his or her campaign committee or group of loyal supporters before going public with them. A candidate must make sure that each issue is important to the majority of voters and that the candidate's response to the issues resonates with the public. Sometimes a candidate might feel that an issue is important, but opinion surveys or the candidate's main supporters might suggest otherwise. In most of those instances, the candidate is usually wrong.

> *A candidate needs a list of issues to run on. That list should be short, and each issue should be briefly stated.*

Are you running for the right office?

When I was a Mayor, I once presided over the annual budget meeting of the City Council which became quite entertaining. After the final vote on the city budget was taken and we were about to adjourn, one of the new council members raised his hand and asked "When do we vote on the school district budget? That's the budget I really want to vote on." When I informed him that the school district budget was solely in the hands of the local board of education, he was surprised and angry. Clearly, he had run for the wrong office.

If your main concerns are with Social Security and the national debt, you can't solve issues with them by running for a seat in your state legislature. If you are running for Congress, a promise to fix local street potholes or see to it that more police officers are patrolling a certain neighborhood aren't issues that you have jurisdiction over.

This might seem elementary, but a candidate must make sure that the office he or she is thinking about running for will meet personal expectations and aspirations.

> *Run for the right office and for the right reasons.*

The Basic Structure of Government in the United States of America

The National Government

The structure of the federal government is dictated by the United States Constitution. The various departments and agencies needed to carry out the functions of the national government are determined by the President and Congress. The federal government is responsible for issues of nation-wide concern, national defense and foreign affairs.

Executive: Elected President, Vice-President. There are several cabinet departments headed by a Secretary, who are appointed by the President, and many independent commissions and agencies that administer and enforce the law.

Legislative: An elected Congress is made up of two houses: a Senate with two members from each state and a House of Representatives with the number of members from each state allocated by each state's proportional population relative to the national population. Senators serve six-year terms and Representatives serve two-year terms.

Judicial: The United States Supreme Court and federal district and appellate courts are appointed by the President with conformation by the United States Senate. Under the current scheme, federal judges are appointed for life or until they retire.

The State Governments

Every state has its own state constitution that dictates the structure of its government. States have a greater impact on domestic governmental functions than the federal government but may have to follow minimum federal guidelines. State governments also determine the structure and functions of local governments within their boundaries.

Executive: The voters in each state elect a Governor, and in most states, a Lieutenant Governor. Each state has departments and agencies that administer policies and programs adopted by the elected government.

Legislative: Elected state legislatures are normally comprised of two houses: A Senate and a lower house called by various names like Assembly, House of Delegates or House of Representatives. The members of both houses at the state level are elected from districts based on population. Nebraska is the exception to this format. The Nebraska Legislature is comprised of only one house, the Nebraska Senate.

Judicial: Each state has its highest court, usually called the State Supreme Court. Under the highest court are district and local courts, depending on a state's constitution or laws. Each state determines how judges are selected, either by appointment or election.

The Local Governments

How local governments are structured and the functions they are responsible for are largely determined by the constitutions and laws in each state. No two states have exactly the same formula for local governments.

County Governments: The legislative control for setting policies at the county level is governed by an elected county board or county commission. In many states the counties have an appointed or elected county administrator or executive who oversees the day-to-day operations of county departments. The voters in most counties across the nation also elect other officers such as sheriff, register of deeds, coroner, county clerk and treasurer.

Local Governments: Usually smaller in area than a county are villages, cities and towns or townships. How they are comprised varies in each state. They usually have an elected executive such as a Mayor, Town Chairman or Village President and an elected governing body.

School Districts: Education in most school districts across the country is in the hands of an elected board of education. The local school board usually appoints a superintendent of schools and principals to administer educational programs and policies and hire staff.

Specialty Districts: State laws allow for the creation of specialty districts at the local level. Organizations such as downtown improvement districts, water and sewer districts, and rural electrification districts are usually governed by an appointed or elected board or commission.

Primary and General Elections

Primary Elections (primaries) are intended to narrow down the field of candidates to the two individuals who will square off in a General Election. For partisan offices in most states, there are separate primaries for each political party on the ballot. There are two types of partisan Primary Elections: open and closed. In an <u>open</u> partisan Primary, anyone can vote in one of the political party primaries without declaring party affiliation or being registered as a member of a particular party. In a <u>closed</u> partisan Primary, only those who are registered as a supporter of a party can vote in their party primary.

In a few states there are "jungle primaries" or "qualifying primaries" for partisan offices. The two candidates that get the most votes, regardless of party affiliation, are advanced to a General Election. Primaries for non-partisan offices are run like this.

In most states and localities, once Primary Elections are over, the two top vote getters in each partisan Primary or the two top vote getters in non-partisan Primary elections face off for a final vote in a General Election. There are a few exceptions…in a few states and local jurisdictions, a winner of a General Election must receive 50% or more of the votes cast, even if it takes a run-off election. In some places a candidate mearly needs to receive a plurality (most votes of any candidate) to win.

> *Primary Elections narrow the field of candidates for an office, generally to two individuals, who then move on to compete in the General Election.*

Do you need to decide on a political party?

For candidates running for a non-partisan local office, party affiliation usually isn't important. If a political party overwhelmingly dominates a non-partisan candidate's community or district, party affiliation may be an advantage even if the party designation isn't on the ballot.

Seeking a partisan office, candidates usually run under the banner of one of the two major political parties or run as an independent. A candidate has a number of factors that to consider in determining which party banner to run under. Which major party does the candidate belong to or generally support? Is there a dominant party in the election district? Is there an incumbent in office who can't lose in a partisan primary election but can be defeated by a candidate from the other party in a general election?

The main advantage of running for a partisan office on a party ticket is that it improves the chances of getting volunteer and financial support. With more and more people identifying as "independent," however, party affiliation may not be as important as it was years ago.

There is a way for a candidate to win an election in an area where his or her party is in the minority. Just don't talk about party affiliation. I won four elections to the Wisconsin Senate in a district that normally voted 2-1 against candidates of my chosen party. In areas where my party was strong, I put party affiliation in my ads. In areas where my party was weak, I left off party affiliation.

> *Party affiliation usually improves the chances of being elected by increasing volunteer and financial support.*

The Differences between the Political Parties

The Democratic and Republican political parties in the United States are less ideological then their counterparts in Europe, although that distinction has been diluted in recent years. In general, the Republican Party is viewed as being more conservative while the Democratic Party is viewed as being more liberal.

Both parties are for jobs, patriotism, strong families, adequate military defense, peace, and prosperity. It's how they pursue achieving those goals where the parties differ. Republicans tend to favor governmental non-interference in free market capitalism while Democrats tend to favor a strong governmental role in overseeing the economy. Republicans tend to favor addressing issues at the local and state levels of government while Democrats tend to favor a strong national government and the establishment of national standards. Republicans tend to be more conservative on issues such as gay rights and abortion while Democrats tend to favor liberalized social policies. Republicans tend to be against higher taxes and increased government spending while Democrats tend to favor higher taxes and more government spending in order to achieve policy objectives.

You will notice that I use the word "tend" a lot and there are several reasons for that. There are conservative and liberal wings of both parties that have more in common with one another than they do with their parent parties. Historically a southern Democrat had more in common with a Republican from Indiana than a fellow Democrat from New York. Candidates often make a choice to affiliate with a political party out of expediency, not political philosophy. Someone might think like a Democrat but run for Sheriff as a Republican only because Republicans dominate the county he or she is running in. Then there is the fact that many issues cannot be labeled as "conservative" or "liberal". If a Democratic Governor in one state proposes clamping down on littering and a Republican Governor in another state proposes that same law, are the proposed laws "conservative" or "liberal"?

In recent years, the Democratic Party has become more ideologically liberal and the Republican Party has become more ideologically conservative. A candidate might affiliate with one of the major political parties, but he or she would be wise to refrain from being either extremely liberal or extremely conservative. Most American voters are not ideologically liberal or conservative, but somewhat in the middle. The middle of the political spectrum is where the most votes are.

Can you pass the "laugh test"?

Once you decide why you want to run, it's time to determine your initial degree of support. If your spouse, the best man at your wedding or your sister thinks you don't stand a chance, then you might want to re-think your candidacy.

Quietly run your candidacy by your closest friends and family. After all, you will need their support to help you organize and run your campaign and to provide seed money to finance your endeavor.

> *If your family and friends don't take your candidacy seriously, then you might want to reconsider your intention to run for political office.*

What are your strengths and weaknesses?

Ask yourself, what is a political campaign and who is a winning candidate? We are taught in elementary school that campaigns are a fight of ideas and principles. The truth is that winning candidates are usually the ones who people most relate to or feel comfortable with; the platforms upon which they are running are often of secondary importance. For the politically astute minority, ideas, and principles matter. For the electoral masses the charisma, physical appearance, and trustworthiness of a candidate matter more.

You don't have to look like a movie star to succeed in politics. It helps, however, if you don't look like a troll. Many former leaders of America would probably not be elected today because of our modern electronic media. Abraham Lincoln had a gift for putting words together but had a high-pitched voice. John Tyler was anything but handsome. President Taft was pictured in campaign posters slimmer than his 350 pound frame. Today, your appearance and how you project yourself does matter.

All humans have their faults. Having once gotten a ticket for speeding or a municipal citation for not mowing your grass would not be a barrier to elective office. Once filing for bankruptcy is not necessarily a problem. If you were ever sentenced for robbery or convicted of fraud, however, you had better look for a different occupation than politics. The bottom line is that if you can't explain yourself out of a previous mistake or problem you probably shouldn't be running for public office.

What do you stand for? OK, you are a nice person, you are passably attractive, you have a nice speaking voice and you have a nice-looking family. What do you want to accomplish if elected? How are you going to attack the issues that matter most to people? What are your positions on the issues that impact the daily lives of the people in your constituency?

Selling yourself as a trustworthy, ethical, likeable person is often more important than issues in successful elections. However, you have to stand for something for those who really are paying attention to the campaign. If you are passionate about an issue that the majority of voters oppose or are not interested in, your position might become a liability.

A person thinking about running for office usually is not the best person to objectively review his or her strengths and weaknesses. A candidate should have others perform that important function. Think about the famous "self-portrait" by the artist Norman Rockwell. He is seen in the painting as looking in a mirror to get some perspectives for his artwork. The person in the mirror is quite ordinary looking. The person on the canvass he is painting looked like a very handsome movie star.

> *A candidate should have others objectively look at his or her strengths and weaknesses.*

Determine the Public Perception of Your Prospective Opponent

An initial essential ingredient that too many small campaigns fail to focus on is an analysis of the public's view of the opposing candidate. Studies have shown that people often vote more *against* someone on the ballot rather than *for* someone. Is your prospective opponent someone that people like, but know is ineffective? Has your opponent taken stands on issues that are politically unpopular? Does your opponent have personal ethical, moral or financial problems?

You can be the best candidate in the world, but if your opponent is likable and viewed with respect, your job of winning is going to be difficult. Remember that for every vote your opponent loses you gain two votes. A major task for your campaign is to gain votes for yourself partly by taking votes away from your opponent.

> *Knowing the strengths and weaknesses of an opponent can be essential for a campaign to be successful.*

You don't have to spend a lot of money in hiring a polling firm to identify the strengths and weaknesses of your opponent. You can get informal polling done through your friends and relatives, i.e. your early supporters. Ask them to talk to people who interact with many people during the day such as the local barber, store managers or the town gossip who is on the phone all day.

Locking up Early Support

If your friends and family support your candidacy, then it's time to broaden your lists of individuals or organizations that you will need to get behind you. If you are running for a partisan office, you will obviously need the support of party leaders. Even if you are running for a non-partisan office, the support of leaders of the party of your political persuasion can be instrumental in garnering financial support and volunteers.

Identify the leaders in the business community, religious and civic organizations, social clubs, and labor unions. Do not assume that the "leader" of a group is necessarily the elected chairmen or president. Often, it's the elder statesman, a dedicated board member or the person who works out compromises who is the true leader.

Once you have compiled a list of leaders, try to make an appointment to visit each of them in person, even before you announce. In the early stages of a campaign season, many leaders may not want to come out and support your candidacy, particularly if you are running against an incumbent. Don't let that offend or worry you. Your initial job is to introduce yourself and ask that they *consider* supporting your candidacy if you decide to run. They will be flattered that you asked. Many of them may volunteer that they will support your candidacy. Get back in touch with these leaders once you have actually announced your candidacy and try to lock in their support.

> *Getting the early support of key individuals is important. They then are committed to a candidate and provide financial support, volunteering and talking up a candidacy in a community.*

Study the Election Laws

Every state has election laws that apply to candidates running for local or state office. In most jurisdictions there are caps on how much a single individual can donate, disclaimer requirements in advertising, and financial reporting requirements to election officials. You and your campaign treasurer should know those limits and requirements backwards and forwards. Violating elections laws can doom your campaign and subject you to fines, having your name stricken from the ballot and even imprisonment.

> *Know the election laws that you will be running under or trouble will come your way.*

Announcing Your Candidacy

By properly following a few basic steps, the announcement of your candidacy can jump-start your campaign. One of the few times the media will give you free publicity is when you actually announce that you are running for office. Plan ahead to do the following on the day you select to announce your candidacy:

- Have an announcement statement ready well ahead of your announcement date. Include with your announcement a close up "head shot" black and white glossy photo. Have the photo done professionally as this will be the photo that the print media will use many times during the campaign.

- If your district is compact and there are limited media outlets, try and visit all newspaper editors and radio and TV news managers on the day of your announcement. If that is not practical, send your announcement out two to three days in advance of your announcement date with the words "For Release (date)" at the top of your statement.

- Keep your announcement short and not over a page and a half, double-spaced. Include a brief statement as to why you are running, some issues that you feel are important and some personal information about your family and career. Do not get too specific on any issues at this time or talk about yourself in a manner that some would interpret as being self-aggrandizing.

- If you are running for a state office or a major local office and you believe the electronic media will cover your announcement, you should consider holding an announcement rally at a strategic location. If you go this route, be sure that you have many supporters in attendance, a backdrop sign with your name and the office you are seeking, refreshments and information packets for all media representatives in attendance.

> ***Work to maximize media exposure in making the announcement of your candidacy.***

Getting Nominated

In most states a candidate must secure a specified number of signatures on nomination papers in order to get on the ballot. The importance of this process is often overlooked by candidates. Never just secure the minimum number of signatures needed. Always strive to get as many signatures as you can with a goal of getting at least three times the number of signatures required. That is important for the following reasons.

- The political landscape is littered with good candidates that did not get on the ballot because of insufficient nomination signatures. In many states even one signature of a person not living in the candidate's district or not registered to vote can result in a whole petition being tossed out.

- People are flattered that you ask them to help you get on the ballot. If a person signs your nomination petition, they will have a tendency to support you later on.

- Make copies of your nomination petitions before turning them in. Send a note to everyone signing your petitions to thank them and ask if they would help you further in getting elected by volunteering in your campaign.

- Turning in more signatures than your opponent gives you "bragging rights." Send out a news release, preferably with a picture of you turning in petitions to election officials. The best way to maximize the number of signatures you collect is for you and your supporters to go door to door in your district. If the election laws in your state allow you to do so, have nomination petitions printed up containing not only the required format, but also your picture and campaign theme at the top of the petition sheet.

Make sure to turn in you petitions to the proper election official by the deadline required to get on the ballot. In fact, turn in your nomination papers a few days in advance of the deadline just to make sure you are not late.

> *Don't overlook the importance of maximizing the number of nomination signatures and turn them in on time.*

Planning For Election Day and the Days before Election Day

What is the sole purpose of a campaign? It is to get enough votes through absentee ballots or ballots cast on Election Day to elect a candidate. To do that, a campaign must concentrate on what it needs to do in the final days and hours of a campaign and work backward and to establish a timeline.

a) Early voting by absentee ballot is allowed in all jurisdictions in the United States. Campaigns can get lists of people requesting absentee ballots by mail at the offices of local election officials. It's important for a campaign to make contact with those absentee voters by phone or mail. Many states allow early voting at government offices a few days prior to Election Day. A few strategically placed campaign yard signs on the streets leading to those polling locations will help a campaign. Some states are experimenting with mail-in ballots and ballots cast electronically. Ads, mailings and phone contacts near

Election Day won't influence early voters since they have already cast their ballots. Early in a campaign a plan needs to be devised to reach early voters or voters casting ballots through non-traditional means.

b) A campaign needs to plan on how to concentrate yard signs on all streets leading to polling stations on Election Day. A campaign must have a plan to get signs legally placed near polling places to give a candidate one last shot at influencing a voter's decision.

c) Getting enough volunteers to hand out literature or hold up signs near polling places is difficult, but those activities can be highly effective. Make sure that election laws and regulations are being followed. In most jurisdictions there are setback restrictions on how close a yard sign placement or literature distribution can occur near a polling place. Violate those requirements and a campaign might get some unfavorable news on the noon newscast with 6-8 hours left for people to cast ballots.

d) As will be discussed in subsequent chapters, a campaign must plan to maximize advertising and direct mailings in the last few days before ballots are cast. Using up available finances too early in a campaign can be devastating.

e) It's important for a candidate and his or her closest advisors to know how to get in touch with one-another immediately to respond to new allegations, issues or attacks right before or on Election Day. It is not unusual for opposing campaigns to employ new offensive maneuvers the last few days of a campaign. A wise candidate must be prepared to respond swiftly, but only after consulting with top advisors and supporters on the best strategy.

f) Some political strategists advise candidates to campaign on Election Day at malls, street corners and factory gates. I do not. Many people do not want to be bothered with a candidate on Election Day and many will think that the candidate is desperate. Rather, I tell candidates to have a good breakfast, go to church if you are inclined, vote and spend the afternoon blowing up balloons and setting tables for the Victory Party. A good thing for a candidate to do on Election Day is to call his or her major volunteers and contributors and thank them for their support.

> *Early in a campaign a candidate and his or her committee should plan for what is going to occur during the last days of the campaign.*

Chapter 2: The Campaign Organization

No matter how large or small your campaign is, you need a campaign organization of committed individuals who want to see you elected. That is important because a campaign organization can be of great value to you in getting various campaign tasks accomplished. It can also serve as an advisory body to you in determining how the campaign should be run, what issues should be talked about, and what activities you personally should focus on to win.

Always Form a Campaign Committee

For a very small race it might not be necessary to have a large campaign committee, particularly if the candidate intends to self-fund his or her own campaign. However, without a committee it looks like a candidate lacks support. That will show up plainly in a disclaimer. A disclaimer like "Authorized and Paid for by Concerned Taxpayers for Jane Smith, Frank Appletree, Treasurer" sounds better than "Authorized and Paid for by Concerned Taxpayers for Jane Smith, Jane Smith, Treasurer."

The formation of a campaign committee is of paramount importance in order to provide structure to a campaign, fulfill legal requirements and disseminate the tasks of the campaign amongst supporters. Even in a small campaign, it is difficult for a candidate to do everything that needs to get done to win.

> *The formation of a campaign committee is of paramount importance.*

Registering Your Campaign Committee

In most jurisdictions, a campaign committee must be registered with the appropriate election officials. For a local office that is usually a municipal or county clerk. For a state office like a seat in the state legislature there is usually an independent elections commission or the state secretary of state's office that registers campaign committees.

Again, know the election laws that apply to the office you are seeking. In many states, for example, candidates or campaign committees are prohibited from accepting any campaign donations or spending any money on the campaign before a campaign committee is registered. Failure to properly register your committee can result in fines and even preventing your name from appearing on the ballot.

In order to register, generally there are three basic requirements: a) the name of the committee, b) a list of its officers (generally just a chairman and a treasurer) and c) the name of the financial institution where your campaign checking account will be kept.

> *Be sure that your campaign committee is properly registered with election officials.*

Disclaimer Requirements and the Use of Union "Bugs"

In most jurisdictions, candidates for local and state office must use a disclaimer in all advertisements and on all signs, literature pieces and handouts. Disclaimers tell the public exactly who is paying for the campaign materials or advertisements. Failure to use a disclaimer can lead to serious penalties. While the exact format may be slightly different, most states require wording such as "Authorized and Paid for by the (committee name), (name and title of Chairman or Treasurer)." Check with your appropriate election official to ascertain what the correct wording needs to be.

If your district is heavily unionized, you should consider having campaign literature and handouts printed in a printing shop that is unionized. That allows you to have a union "bug" printed on your campaign materials. A "bug" is just a tiny logo of the local printer's union that is usually placed at the end of your disclaimer. Most people wouldn't notice it. Strong union supporters will be looking for it.

> *Most election laws require a disclaimer in all advertising and campaign materials.*

Selecting a Campaign Name

The name of your campaign committee is used for registering your committee with election officials, meeting disclaimer requirements and to get your name or campaign theme out to the public.

You could select something as boring as "Fitzgerald for Council Committee" or "Authorized and Paid for by the Jones for State Senate Committee", but why? Why not use your committee name to get a campaign theme or message out? Why not use your name in a clever way to get voters to chuckle a little, associate something positive with your candidacy or remember your name? Instead of "Authorized and Paid for by the Smith for Council Committee, Joe Flowerpot, Chairman", why not "Authorized and Paid for by the Smith of Progressive Change Committee…" or "Authorized and Paid for by the Smith Ethics in Government Committee…" or "Authorized and Paid for by People United to Clean Up City Hall Committee…" ?

> **Come up with a committee name that sends a message to voters.**

Your Campaign Slogan

While your committee name should send a message, your campaign slogan is more important in that regard. Your slogan should be used on all literature, handouts, and advertisements. It's the one message that needs to make a statement as to why you are running or why you are the better candidate. Sometimes a slightly humorous slogan does the trick too. The important thing about the slogan is that it needs to grab people's attention. Why do you think that large corporations spend so much money coming up with their advertising slogans?

I once advised a successful candidate who was running against an individual who was generally perceived as holding political views that were out of the mainstream. We came up with a slogan of "Responsible, Not Radical." We didn't come out and say that the other candidate was politically radical, but the slogan implied that our candidate was responsible, and that the other candidate represented some fringe element.

I advised another candidate whose first name was June. The slogan for that campaign was "June In November". She won handily against a popular incumbent in a district that normally voted 2-1 against candidates of her party affiliation.

In my first successful run for a legislative seat I used a theme that was somewhat humorous. I was 25 years old and virtually unknown. At the time there was an ad for the pain reliever Alka-Seltzer that used the slogan "Try It, You Will Like It." We did a take-off of that with my campaign theme of "Try Me, You'll Like Me". People laughed, but they remembered the slogan and the candidate. I couldn't have asked for more.

Whether you are trying to get a serious message out or use humor, don't overlook the importance of selecting a good campaign slogan. Brainstorm with your close supporters over what your slogan should be. Once you decide your slogan, don't change it.

A campaign slogan must send a message or create an image.

Campaign Colors

If you are going to use signs of any kind like billboards, bumper stickers and yard signs, your campaign needs to select campaign colors. It's alright to have the lettering on a campaign sign in a bright color such as red, orange or florescent green. Don't use such bright colors for the background color, however, because that tends to get too bright for most eyes to tolerate. Greens, blues and red, white and blue are always acceptable.

If your name has a color reference in it, take advantage of that fact. If your name is Joe Brown what logical color are you going to use in campaign signs? I once advised a candidate whose first name was Iris. Her campaign signs contained the iris flower with a background in the color hue of iris.

Is there a color scheme for a local athletic team that you could borrow? If you only have one team in your district it could be productive to adopt the team's colors. If there are several competing teams in your district, however, that could be disastrous. I live in Green Bay, Wisconsin. The green and gold colors of our Green Bay Packer football team are often borrowed in local campaigns.

Whatever campaign colors that you select, stay with that color scheme on all signs, ads and printed materials. You want voters to associate your colors with your campaign.

> *Choose campaign colors that stand out or are pleasing to the eye. Use the same colors on all signs, ads and printed materials.*

Official Committee Officers

For legal purposes, such as registering your committee or meeting disclaimer requirements, you need to have official officers of your campaign committee. Generally, only a committee Chairperson and a committee Treasurer need to be named. Of those two officers, the Treasurer is often the most important person for the operation of the campaign.

Your Treasurer needs to be a trusted friend with the ability to keep accurate records. The Treasurer needs to be sure that campaign contributions and disbursements are properly and accurately recorded for in making campaign reports to election officials. I have seen some campaigns having the candidate or the candidate's spouse as the Treasurer. That is a mistake for two reasons: a) the candidate and the candidate's spouse should be meeting voters, not taking care of financial reports, writing checks and depositing contributions and b) by not having a third party as Treasurer it looks to the public like the candidate does not have broad support.

The campaign Chairperson may or may not oversee the campaign. Often the Chairperson merely "lends" his or her good name to the campaign by way of an endorsement. The Chairperson should be a respected leader in the community to give credence to your campaign. The Chairperson may wish to manage the campaign, but more often he or she is just a trusted advisor.

If your district constitutes a large geographical area with multiple media outlets, you may want to consider designating an official of your campaign in each region to "localize" your campaign. That individual's name would appear on disclaimers in advertising in each region. When I ran for the State Senate in Wisconsin my district was large and was made up of three State Representative districts. In one State Representative district the name of my campaign Chairperson appeared on disclaimers because he lived there. In another district, a locally popular lady's name appeared as Treasurer. In the third State Representative district the name of a well-known local businesswoman was designated as "Vice-Chairperson" of the campaign. The more you can "localize" the names of prominent individuals in disclaimers the better. True, some of those "official officers" of your campaign may not do a lot of the grunt work, but their names serve as a local endorsement for your candidacy.

> *At a minimum, your Committee needs a Chairperson and a Treasurer.*

Your Working Campaign Committee

Now that you have established your "official" officers for legal purposes, it's time to select the "worker bees" of your campaign. Listed below are some suggested leadership positions for your campaign. If your district is geographically small or your campaign low-key or uncomplicated you can get by with one individual holding each position for your whole election district or even taking on multiple functions. On the other hand, if your district is geographically large or your campaign is complicated you might want to have some of these positions filled on an area basis. In a multi-county district, for example, you might want to have a Coffee Coordinator or a Finance Coordinator in each county. The more you can localize your campaign the better.

Here are some positions you should think about filling in your campaign organization:

- Campaign Manager: This person may or may not be your official campaign Chairperson. The Manager must be a politically savvy friend who you can trust to give you the truth and who is unafraid to bat you on the head if he or she thinks you are doing something wrong. The Manager must have the authority to run the campaign in every detail so that you can concentrate on what you need to be doing...meeting the voters.

- Publicity Coordinator: This person needs to know how to write news releases and what issues will "grab" the attention of voters. If you can enlist the support of a local reporter that would be ideal. This individual should prepare news releases in advance of a speaking event and be responsible for disseminating those releases to the media throughout your district. An added plus would be if your Publicity Coordinator has photographic skills and can send in a picture with a news release.

- Advertising Coordinator: This is a very key position. While you will rely on your Publicity Coordinator to get you "free" exposure in the media, the Advertising Coordinator is responsible for the "paid" messages and images you want to get out to the voters. The Advertising Coordinator needs to know the rate costs and deadlines for ads in each media outlet, how to put effective ads together and work with your Treasurer in sending ads and checks to media outlets on a timely basis.

- Technology and Information Coordinator: Most campaigns would be well served to have a person with an information or digital technology background. That person should be in charge of breaking down poll lists for mailings, canvassing and voter targeting. He or she could also oversee the candidate's exposure in social media and managing a web site.

- Materials Coordinator: Who is going to distribute your yard signs, flyers, and handouts? If you have a geographically large district that task can be huge. You need a volunteer who will deliver campaign materials throughout your district. I made a bad mistake in my first campaign in an eight-county district of not having a volunteer to deliver yard signs in each community. I ended up spending days driving hundreds of miles to deliver signs when I should have been spending the time meeting voters.

- Schedule Coordinator: Every well-run campaign needs to have someone to schedule your campaign activities so that you are making the best use of your time and are not expected to be in two places at once. This person should schedule you into speaking events, parades, community fairs, media interviews and the like. You need to give your Schedule Coordinator the times that you are available and rely on this person to organize the efficient use of your time. This position is a good opportunity for your spouse, sibling or "significant other", who knows your habits and schedule already, to make a very valuable contribution to your campaign.

- Finance Coordinator: The selection of this individual is extremely important to your campaign. Without good financing, your campaign is going nowhere. Work with your Finance Coordinator to form a Finance Committee which can assist in raising funds for your campaign. If your election district is geographically large, you may want to have a Finance Coordinator and a Finance Committee in several regions.

- Coffee Coordinator: A Coffee Coordinator should work to schedule "coffees" or small receptions in the homes of influential people in your district. Again, if your district is geographically large you might want to have different people fulfill this responsibility in each region of your district. This person needs to find out from the Schedule Coordinator when you will be available to do coffees. A good tactic is to schedule several one-hour coffees in a specific area on the same evening or weekend afternoon.

- Volunteer Coordinator: The Volunteer Coordinator is

responsible for recruiting volunteer helpers for your campaign. Going door-to-door, passing out literature, addressing mailings, yard sign distributions, and event set-ups are some of the things that volunteers can do.

- Events Coordinator: This person should concentrate on events that raise money for the campaign or provide opportunities for the candidate to meet voters. The Events Coordinator should work closely with the Finance Coordinator to plan and execute fundraising events like cocktail receptions, sit down dinners and informal events like spaghetti feeds and picnics. The Events Coordinator might also be employed to organize non-fundraising events such as campaign rallies or bus tours.

> *It is critical to have coordinators to take on the responsibilities for the various functions of a campaign. In a large constituency or a complicated race, consider appointing such coordinators on a regional basis.*

Advisory Committees

You might want to consider the formation of "advisory committees" to your campaign that: a) advice you on specific issues of your campaign, b) form a nucleus of support within specific groups of voters, and c) assist in identifying potential contributors or volunteers for your campaign within each group.

I witnessed several campaigns in which "advisory committees" were used quite effectively to publicize support for a candidate. Even if such committees only meet with the candidate once or twice, their members may be able to feed a campaign important information, help plan campaign strategy and give leads in gaining financial and endorsement support with other members of the voter group represented by the advisory committee.

A campaign may want advisory committees based on the major segments in the constituency of the candidate: business, labor, farmers, health professionals, etc.

If nothing else, sending out a news release announcing the formation and membership of such "advisory committees" sends a message that the campaign has broad support and that the candidate is hearing the views of diverse members of the electorate.

> *Consider forming "advisory committees" to garner input and support from specific segments of the electorate.*

Use of the Internet and Social Media

Is your campaign going to have a web site? If so, get one established early in the campaign. Include lots of pictures, a brief rundown of your issues and information on how readers might volunteer or contribute. Provide a few key points about your qualifications and experience. Most visitors to your website will not want to spend hours reading an in-depth analysis of current issues, so use this opportunity to provide personality and likability images of you with only a few short messages on issues.

It is imperative today to also have an email address for supporters and voters to be able to reach you directly. DO NOT use your personal email address as your campaign email address. Make sure that the addresses of a web page and your email address have your name and the office you seek. For example, a domain name like www.Flathead4Senate.com and an email address like Bob@Flathead4Senate.com, reinforces your name and the office you are seeking.

You should consider utilizing other forms of electronic platforms such as Facebook™, Twitter™, and YouTube™ to get your message across and reach a broader, more connected audience, particularly younger voters. These platforms must be used with care. There have been many instances in recent years of a candidate or elected official inadvertently ending a promising career by quickly sending out a message that cannot be retrieved. Remember that once a photo, opinion, email, video, tweet™ or other communication leaves your computer or phone it will be available to the entire world to see in perpetuity. Always be sure to separate personal and campaign related communications. You should even consider getting a separate phone and computer just for your campaign.

You or a volunteer should read and, at the very least, acknowledge any electronic platform contact with a response and a thank you message. While a basic tally of issues or concerns raised in these communications can be done by nearly anyone, a larger campaign might wish to hire a specialist to "mine" the data for more valuable insights. The outpouring of the concerns, hopes, and opinions from the people you hope to represent can be a valuable resource in helping to craft your message and plan your campaign.

Some people will leave messages cutting you or your positions to shreds. Don't worry about them and don't get into a back and forth argument with them. Voters expressing a vehement distaste for you or your positions are not likely to change their minds come election time.

Whatever array of internet and social media you employ, use the opportunity to use these technologies to accomplish a number of tasks. Sure, you want to use Facebook and your web site to talk about issues and provide information on how voters can volunteer to help or make donations. Why not also use new technologies to broadcast news releases, announce fundraising events and provide your schedule of campaign appearances on a weekly basis?

> *Use email, your website and social networking platforms to stay in touch with supporters and volunteers and to broaden the reach of your candidacy to voters. Be sure to keep your personal and campaign contact addresses separate.*

Recruiting Volunteers

Regardless of the size of your campaign, you need volunteers to help your various coordinators accomplish their goals. There are many ways to recruit volunteers:

- Start with friends and family. They can serve as your core of volunteers.

- If you are running for a partisan office or are considered to be affiliated with a political party have your Volunteer Coordinator contact party activists.

- As was mentioned in the last chapter, reach out to people who signed your nomination papers. Thank them again for their support and see if they would volunteer in their community to help you.

- Place ads in area media inviting people to join your campaign. You probably won't get too many volunteers this way, but it will get your name out and people will feel warmly toward your campaign in that you are inviting everyone to participate.

- If you have a strong supporter who is a member of a service club, veterans' organization, garden club, church group or professional society ask that person to talk up your candidacy in his or her group and see to see if other people interested in helping.

- Are there political clubs in your local high schools or colleges? If so, their members are already politically attuned. Young people are often the best volunteers because of their energy and enthusiasm.

Recruiting volunteers is very important for a campaign of any size.

Chapter 3: Budget and Finance

A person can be the best candidate for a public office, but if that candidate does not have the financial resources to get his or her message and name before the public, it might not matter. It is essential to prepare a realistic budget, allocate financial resources wisely and have a strategy for raising the funds needed for a campaign to be effective.

Campaign Depository

A campaign must set up a checking account. Obviously, it is preferable that such a financial institution be in the candidate's district. Sometimes that is required by law. The account address and the address on the checks should be that of the campaign Treasurer, not the candidate. A financial institution should be selected that is friendly to the candidate or the Treasurer or is highly respected in the district. In many states and jurisdictions, a campaign must have a checking account before accepting contributions or making expenditures.

> **Open a checking account for your campaign early.**

Contribution Limits

Most jurisdictions limit individual campaign contributions and prohibit corporate or labor union donations. In the 2010 Supreme Court decision in *Citizens United vs. Federal Election Commission*, the court didn't lift bans or caps on direct corporate and labor union donations to campaigns for federal offices. It lifted restrictions on corporate and labor union spending on elections <u>independent</u> of campaigns. In most jurisdictions if a check comes with "Inc." or "LLC" on it the Treasurer should return it and ask the donor to make a personal, non-business campaign contribution.

The United States Supreme Court ruled in *Buckley vs. Valeo* that government cannot impose contribution limits on how much a <u>candidate</u> can give to his or her OWN campaign. The court said, however, that government can limit how much individuals other than the candidate can contribute.

Almost all states (and some local governments) have limits on how much a person, other than the candidate, can contribute to a campaign. The candidate, the Finance Coordinator and the Treasurer must know those limits. Accepting contributions greater than the legal limits can have serious legal consequences and give the opposition an issue that could have been avoided.

In addition to limits on individual contributions and prohibitions on direct corporate and union donations, many election laws limit what a candidate can receive from political parties, the campaign committees of other candidates and Political Action Committees. Make sure the Campaign Treasurer strictly adheres to the limitations. The campaign may have to report that the Treasurer returned donations that went beyond legal limitations, or which were illegal to accept in the first place.

> *In most states and jurisdictions, there are restrictions on contributions. Make sure those regulations are thoroughly understood.*

Public Campaign Financing

In some states there are opportunities for part of a campaign's expenditures to be funded through public campaign financing. The sources of those funds are often "good government" check-offs on state income tax returns. Generally, public financing is limited to legislative and statewide partisan races, not local races.

There are pros and cons of accepting public campaign financing:

- If you accept public campaign financing, you are generally subjected to limits on total contributions and expenditures. If your opponent doesn't accept public financing and has good financial resources, that could be disastrous to your campaign.

- Incumbents usually have a financial advantage over challengers. If you are challenging an incumbent and your campaign is strapped for money maybe accepting public campaign financing is a way for you to "level the playing field".

- Good government types and the general public hate the enormous amounts being spent on campaigns. If you are an under-funded, non-incumbent candidate, that could work to your advantage. You can make an issue in your campaign that you have accepted limits in contributions and expenditures and that your opponent is "trying to buy the election".

- If you accept public campaign financing and subsequently violate contributions and expenditure limits, even inadvertently, you could be required to pay back part or all of the public financing money you received and still be subject to legal limits. If that happens, you will be worse off than if you never agreed to accept the assistance in the first place.

- There is generally little incentive for an incumbent to accept public financing because of the usual financial advantages that an incumbent has. However, if an incumbent is facing a challenger with unusually large financial resources there might be an advantage for an incumbent to consider public campaign financing.

- Public campaign financing programs generally require a candidate to reach a "threshold" of non-public campaign contribution income to qualify. Make sure that your campaign will be able to reach those thresholds before agreeing to being tied to contribution and expenditure limits that are required for public campaign financing.

> *Public financing of campaigns is sometimes available, but it comes with restrictions.*

Campaign Budget

The candidate, the Chairperson, the Campaign Manager, the Finance Coordinator, and the Treasurer all need to work together to devise a realistic campaign budget. In the early stages of a campaign it's hard to know precisely how much money a campaign will have so it is wise to budget on the conservative side.

When making up a budget, "budget backwards." That is, make sure to reserve most of the funds for the end of the campaign when the campaign really needs to spend the most in reaching out to voters. Running short on money for advertising during the last two weeks of the campaign because you spent too much at the beginning of the campaign can spell disaster.

When planning your budget, you need to form a timeline when expenditures will be made for specific priorities in your campaign. That timeline will dictate the fundraising goals that your Finance Coordinator(s) will have to try to meet. Again, be realistic and conservative. If you have a lot more money than anticipated at the end of the campaign you always can dump more dollars into advertising.

For purposes of example, the following could serve as a budget for a race for a county-wide office in a fall election. The format that you use is less important than the fact that the candidate and leaders of the campaign have thought through the anticipated expenditures and income for an effective campaign. Importantly, this budget shows some target dates for raising money.

> *"Budget backwards" and make sure that you have sufficient funds for the end of the campaign.*

Projected Expenditures*:

Campaign Expenditure	Unit Cost	Total Cost	Financing Deadline
Post card mailings	$0.40 each	$4,000 (10,000)	October 15
Media			
a) Daily Horn	$12/column inch	$3,600 (300 column inches)	October 1
b) Weekly Digest	$8/ column inch	$1,600 (200 column inches)	October 1
c) Radio ABCD	$30/ 30 seconds	$1,500 (50 ads)	October 1
Mileage	$0.35/mile	$525 (1,500 mi)	August 15
Yard signs	$4.60 each	$920 (200 signs)	August 1
Billboards	$575 each	$2,875 (5 signs)	July 1
Flyers	$0.55 each	$3,300 (6,000)	June 1
Small handout cards	$0.07 each	$140 (2,000)	June 1
Event costs	Various	$2,500 (1k/1.5k)	June 1/ Oct. 15
	Total:	$20,960	

*These numbers are shown only for example. Costs will vary greatly by location and when a campaign occurs.

Income Timetable:

Target Date	Amount Needed	Likely Fund Sources
June 1-Oct.15 (events)	$2,500	Fundraising events
June 1	$3,440	Candidate family/friends
July 1	$2,875	Two small informal events
August 1	$920	Solicitations
August 15	$525	Solicitations
October 1	$6,700	Solicitations/cocktail event
October 15	$4,000	Solicitations/ dinner
	Total: 20,960	

Initial Campaign Contributions

In almost every campaign, large or small, the candidate and his friends and family need to make contributions for "seed money" to get the campaign going.

One cautionary note: it's OK for a candidate to contribute

a small amount of "seed money" to his or her campaign. If, however, his or her personal contribution is substantial, that could backfire. It looks better to the voting public if the candidate's own contribution is minimal. If all or a significant portion of a campaign is financed by the candidate, it may appear that the candidate really doesn't have much support and that he or she is "trying to buy the election."

The reality check for a campaign is this: unless a candidate's relatives and close friends are willing to give the campaign "up front" contributions, maybe the candidate shouldn't be running at all.

> *Initial contributions need to come from the candidate and his or her friends and relatives.*

How Much Is Too Much OR Too Little?

Whether it is you personally or a member of your finance committee who is asking for money, it's important to: a) ascertain how much a potential donor is capable of giving, and b) actually state a desired amount to the potential donor when asking for a contribution. I once made a mistake of asking a wealthy individual for a contribution but didn't ask for a dollar amount that I knew he was capable of giving. I thought he would offer at least $300. Wrong. After an hour of answering his questions he said that he would send me a check. The $10 check arrived two days later.

Once the campaign has established how much each potential donor is capable of contributing, always ask for more. "Sally, I really appreciate your support for my candidacy, but I really could use some financial help. I would really appreciate it if you would contribute $500 toward my campaign." "Oh, I couldn't go that high," says Sally. "But I could contribute $400."

If your goal was to get a $200 contribution from Sally you are ahead of the game.

> *Potential contributors should be asked to donate more than a "target" level of support.*

Fundraising Events

Some fundraising events raise a great deal of money. Others are designed more to get a candidate's name before the voters. Here are a few examples:

- Picnic-Type Events: These events don't generate a lot of cash, but they are a good way for a candidate to mingle with voters. Ticket prices are kept to a minimum. They will often feature beer and brats, corn roasts, spaghetti dinners, chili cook-offs and the like. They frequently are held in conjunction with a county fair or community event. The important thing with these events is not to raise a lot of money but to get the candidate before the public to meet ordinary citizens and recruit volunteers.

- Sit-Down Dinners: Unless a campaign has a big-name speaker that can demand a high ticket price, sit down dinners are difficult to organize and barely break even. Many voters are not going to spend a large amount of money for a dinner to hear some politician speak unless they are already really committed to your campaign. When the campaign deducts the cost of the hall rental, the meal, advertising, entertainment and decorations, it might be best to skip the sit-down dinner. However, if you have a big-name speaker that can draw a crowd and demand a high ticket price, such an event can be financially rewarding.

- Coffees and Receptions: Low-key events at the homes of supporters do not generally raise a lot of money. They are more intended to have a candidate connect with the voters. Don't miss the opportunity, however, to make a solicitation for funds or to pass out financial support pledge cards at such events.

- Cocktail Receptions: These events are generally geared toward solicitations of business and professional people who are capable of making larger contributions. A "host committee" of prominent community leaders with their names printed in an invitation is beneficial. Written invitations should be followed up by a phone contact a day or two after the invitations arrive in the mail. Cocktail receptions are fairly easy to organize and require minimal costs. Lasting an hour after business hours at a convenient location, cocktail receptions can bring in substantial sums of money. In order to be successful, however, the people invited should be committed to be in attendance and agree to contribute a minimum set donation. Having a popular figure to serve as a "draw" and to say some brief kind words on the candidate's behalf can ensure that the event is successful.

> *Some "fundraising" events raise little or no money but are designed to get the candidate and voters together. A few events to raise larger contributions should be well-planned.*

Personal Solicitations

While a campaign needs some fundraising events to raise money and connect the candidate with voters, nothing is more effective in raising money for a small campaign than personal solicitations. Whether a solicitation is made directly by the candidate or by the Finance Committee members, most of a campaign's budget usually will need to be funded through this technique.

The candidate should sit down with the Finance Committee members and draft a master list of potential contributors. Each member should select names on that master list to contact. Most of the time people will volunteer to contact people they know. Sometimes it helps if a respected person in a profession contacts other members of his or her profession (i.e., a doctor contacting other doctors).

Before making any contacts for funds, each solicitor should have a basic understanding of why the candidate is running and how he or she stands on certain key issues in the district or community. Sometimes a potential contributor really wants to know how the candidate stands on an issue and the person making the solicitation doesn't know the answer. In that case, it's best for the solicitor to volunteer to get the answer from the candidate before actually asking for a donation.

Solicitations in person are preferable to solicitations over the phone. That is particularly true when seeking a substantially large contribution from an individual. Some members of your Finance Committee will be just too busy to make personal visits to potential donors on their list and making contacts by phone is the only thing they can volunteer to do. Respect that.

Finance Committee members need to be direct and unafraid to get to the point. After a few pleasantries, a solicitor should say something like: "George, I am supporting the campaign of Mary Birchtree. I think that Mary would be an outstanding public official. My purpose in contacting you today is to ask you to help Mary get elected by making a $500 contribution to her campaign. Can I count on you for that?"

As stated above, solicitors should know how much a potential financial supporter is capable of contributing and always ask for more. The Finance Committee needs to discuss how much each potential contributor on your master list is capable of donating. Always keep in mind, however, that in most jurisdictions there are limits on how much an individual can contribute.

The Finance Committee should determine the timing of in-person and phone solicitations so that each member knows when their fundraising needs to be done. The Finance Coordinator should contact each member of the committee frequently to ascertain how the solicitations are going and act on opportunities for improvement.

Contributions made to the campaign through personal solicitations should be made out by check to the campaign committee but sent to, or picked up by, the Finance Committee member who made the solicitation. In that way, fundraising solicitors can keep track of the collection of checks and get back to anyone who previously made a pledge but didn't forward the contribution.

> *In most cases, personal solicitations are the most productive means of raising needed cash to run an effective political campaign.*

Use Your Imagination

You would be surprised how some imaginative activities can result in productive fundraising. You and your Finance Committee or Campaign Committee should brainstorm on innovative ideas to bring funds into your campaign. Sometimes even if an idea only breaks even, it can generate visibility and favorable publicity. Here are a few examples:

- During my second campaign for the Wisconsin State Senate my wife came up with the idea of manufacturing and selling "limited edition" buttons with our theme during that campaign of "I Know Theno". I thought that she was crazy. I finally relented (husbands do that frequently even if they are in high public office). We hired an agency that employed persons with disabilities to manufacture 1,000 three-inch-wide buttons. We placed ads in local papers that promised to send a "limited edition" Theno button for a contribution of $10 or more. Well, my wife was right. We quadrupled our contribution "take" over the cost of advertising and making the buttons.

- One candidate that I advised offered to do a half day of yard work for the highest bidder for his services. While the candidate lost a Saturday afternoon, he gained $1,500 for his campaign.

- I have witnessed several campaigns offering raffles at fundraising events for prizes ranging from a donated new lawn tractor to a roast pig. Before offering a raffle for a fundraiser make sure that such an activity is legal in your state or jurisdiction. If you can do raffles legally, they are great fundraisers and fun for participants.

- Silent auctions have proven effective in some campaigns. Have some of you major supporters donate nice items to auction off at an event. You will be surprised at the income you derive. Again, check with election officials to ascertain if such activities are legal in securing campaign contributions

> *Many imaginative ways to raise money actually pay off.*

Political Action Committees

Many business, labor unions and professional organizations have a Political Action Committee (PAC) that their members contribute toward. Financial support from PACs is given to candidates that support the political goals of the parent organization. Often, a contribution from a PAC to a candidate comes with a formal endorsement.

Financial support from PACs can be a blessing and can be a curse, or both! By accepting a PAC contribution and the implicit or explicit endorsement from an organization, the campaign is acknowledging that the candidate supports the political goals of that organization. If those goals are something the candidate really believes in and can justify to the voters, then go right ahead and accept a PAC donation. On the other hand, if the goals of the PAC-funding organization are something the candidate has trouble with or which are not popular in the election district, a candidate might want to have second thoughts about accepting donations from such a group.

In one of my campaigns we accepted a donation from an organization that we knew nothing about. It turned out that the group was a radical, fringe organization that espoused views that I did not agree with. My opponent had a "field day" criticizing me for being supported by the organization in question. I ended up returning the donation, but the public relations damage had already been done.

Acquiring support from a PACs can provide a campaign with large sums of money in a short period of time with very little effort. Just make sure that the campaign is following restrictions on PAC contributions in your state or jurisdiction. Election laws in many places have caps on how much individual PACs can contribute toward a campaign. There may also be caps on the aggregate amount of money your campaign can accept from PACs, particularly if the candidate is accepting public financing.

> *If a campaign accepts campaign contributions from PACs it is implied that the candidate supports the positions of the organizations that the money comes from.*

Giving Thanks

Contributors to a campaign are people who invested their financial resources toward your political future. A candidate should make sure to send contributors a thank-you note. Contributors will be appreciative of the gesture and will become more enthusiastic supporters and more willing to donate in the future.

There are a few variations to this recommendation: a) people who contribute $5 or another small amount to your campaign by buying an item (hotdog, brat, button, etc.) at a low-key event need not receive a thank you and b) if there are a large number of reasonably substantial contributions, the campaign might want to set a dollar threshold of when the candidate personally sends a thank you note and when the Treasurer sends out such a message on the candidate's behalf.

Whoever is sending out a thank you note, the sender should write a personal, handwritten message. That has a bigger impact than something that is mass printed. Having the campaign photo or logo on the face of the card or letter is a good idea in re-connecting the contributor to the campaign.

> *A short thank you note to contributors is important.*

Chapter 4: Media Relations and Free Publicity

A candidate's relations with the local media and how his or her campaign allocates funds in media advertising most often determines the outcome of an election. A wise candidate should strive to get "free publicity" or "earned media" through media interviews, letters to the editor, web sites, social network pages, blogs and news releases as well as "paid publicity" through a coordinated advertising campaign.

Establish Media Relations Early

Even before a candidate announces that he or she is running for office, it would do well for the candidate to visit with newspaper editors and electronic media managers. If nothing else, these encounters could be merely "courtesy visits" for the candidate to introduce himself. Be mindful that editors and media managers might not be the people a candidate ultimately needs to establish a personal, professional relationship with at media outlets. Establishing a good relationship with a reporter of a local newspaper might bring a candidate more dividends than actually having a connection with the editor.

During initial media visits a candidate shouldn't be surprised if he is asked how much the campaign will be advertising with the media outlet. A wise candidate would be evasive! The candidate should say that he hopes to advertise as much as possible in the outlet, depending on the campaign's financial resources.

In some instances, media outlets will give preferential treatment to news releases and advertising space to a particular candidate because the outlet supports that individual. It must be remembered that a local newspaper or radio station is a business. If the manager of a local media outlet senses that the outlet will not profit or will lose business by helping a campaign, the manager might shy away from giving a candidate "free publicity" as well as assistance in positioning "paid" advertisements.

A wise former campaign Chairperson of mine (and a former newspaper columnist) advised me that the most important person at a newspaper was the nameless guy in the back of the printing shop who determined headlines. A headline of "Joe Flowerpot Proposes New Initiative on Crime Prevention" has more impact for a campaign than "Alternative Crime Prevention Discussed."

> *A candidate should develop professional friendships with media people early in the campaign.*

The Format of Printed News Releases

There is a real skill in developing good political news releases. Having a Publicity Chairman who is able to write effective news releases could be a key to a campaign's success. Remember, when news releases are printed or broadcast, they are considered "free publicity." They should grab the attention of voters and not be too lengthy.

I would recommend the following in issuing news releases from a campaign:

- Place a date at the top of your release such as: "For Release, 1:00 PM, Tuesday, August 24". That signals to reporters, editors and managers that a candidate doesn't expect them to release his or her comments before that date and time. Most media outlets will respect that deadline. If a media outlet wants to "scoop" other outlets (which they will try to do with some regularity) before that release time, a candidate would be well advised to say nothing before the appointed hour. Favoring one media outlet over another can only bring a campaign a basket of trouble.

- Suggest a headline at the top of the page in the release. Media outlets may not use the suggestion, but it gets them thinking. A headline like "Jane Doe Speaks Out on Fiscal Responsibility" has more appeal than "Candidate Addresses Garden Club." A candidate's name should always appear in a suggested headline.

- Print a dateline at the beginning of the candidate's news release to indicate the community in which the candidate spoke. Have that community's name in caps, i.e., "MAPLEVILLE-Frank Tulip, candidate for State Representative, told an audience in Mapleville that if elected he would fight for..."

- The candidate's name should be in the first sentence of any news release, i.e. "Pete Alarmclock, candidate for city council, said today that..." Some media outlets will "cut and crop" a political release. Others will print or read a release verbatim. Make sure your name is one of the first things that people hear or read.

- A good news release should hit the main points that a candidate wants to get across to voters in the first paragraph. It should be hard hitting and succinct. Most readers or listeners "tune out" after initial comments unless the subject of the release is extraordinarily interesting or important.

- A candidate must remember to not get overly complicated in a news release. Public policy issues can be extremely complex. A candidate shouldn't even try to explain the intricacies of a complicated issue but concentrate his or her comments on one facet that will grab the attention of voters.

- A Publicity Coordinator must make sure that the candidate's name is mentioned in every paragraph at least once. The name should appear in the news release as often as possible without impeding the flow of the text. What is a campaign trying to do with news releases? It is trying to get the candidate's name across to voters and to articulate issues. The candidate won't be articulating issues after the election, however, if he or she doesn't get good name recognition.

- A campaign should <u>never</u> send out a news release beyond a page and a half. Newspaper editors and electronic media managers are not going to transmit to voters (free) an encyclopedia of a candidate's thoughts on the origins of the universe. Preferably, a news release should be less than one side of a sheet of paper.

> *News releases must be short and mention the candidate's name often.*

How, When and Where to Issue News Releases

Here are a few time-tested suggestions on the "how, when and where" of sending out news releases for a campaign:

- Most media outlets will not print or broadcast a news release unless a candidate's comments in the release are given before a legitimate audience. That's where the Scheduling Coordinator and the Publicity Coordinator need to work together. The Scheduling Coordinator should book a candidate into a speaking event and then inform the Publicity Coordinator that an event has been scheduled. It's up to the candidate and the Publicity Coordinator to then agree on an appropriate news release.

- Speaking events which justify a news release do not necessarily have to be before 1,000 people. Depending on the characteristics of the district and the nature of the local media, a campaign might be able to issue a news release after the candidate talks to 10 people at a neighborhood coffee reception. Local service clubs are particularly appropriate venues because they involve community leaders who meet regularly.

- Ideally, one news release should be sent out each week after a candidate announces his or her candidacy. A campaign might get by with sending out two releases per week if there is some burning issue, but that is stretching it. Unless your race is the only game in town, remember that candidates in other races and your opponent are struggling to get the same free media exposure as your campaign.

- A campaign would be wise to issue news releases at different locations in the constituency every time the candidate speaks. That will drive the opponent crazy and will demonstrate to the media and the public that the candidate is reaching out to every area and group in the election district.

- A candidate should have a news release prepared in advance of a speaking event. The page or page and a half news release might amount to only five minutes of a twenty-minute presentation before the local organization, but the candidate needs to deliver its contents to give credence to the release. One candidate who I tried to help didn't mention a subject in a talk she gave but included that topic in a news release. It so happened that the local newspaper editor was in the audience. The editor was not too pleased and said so in an editorial. Ouch!

- News releases should be sent out only after the candidate had delivered his or her talk at a speaking event. Hey, a candidate could be killed in a car accident, be sick in bed or tied up in traffic and not able to give the talk upon which the news release is based. The campaign should mail, email or FAX a news release when it is clear that the issues covered in the release were actually spoken about at a legitimate speaking event.

- Most news releases today are sent out electronically. If the campaign is going to send a news release through regular mail, send it from the community where the candidate spoke. That way, the post mark verifies that the candidate was in the community that the dateline says he or she was at. In the days before email, I always had a bundle of envelopes (stuffed with my release, stamped and addressed) to district-wide media that I mailed from a local post office immediately following a speaking event.

- The electronic media can transmit a candidate's message instantaneously after they receive it. Daily newspapers usually can print releases the day following receipt. Shoppers and weekly newspapers are another story. Many of these publications come out on a Thursday or Friday. Sometimes they need to have releases by Monday or Tuesday for printing. The Publicity Coordinator needs to know printing deadlines for weekly newspapers and shoppers if a news release needs to get included in a specific edition.

> *News releases should be based on actual talks by the candidate before legitimate forums. They should be sent to the media only after a speaking event.*

Letters to the Editor

People do read "Letter to the Editor" columns in newspapers. Sure, some comments that appear in a local paper are spontaneous. More often than not, however, letters are encouraged or even "manufactured" by candidates during campaigns. Newspaper editors understand that and are therefore skeptical about letters that arrive on their desks during the campaign season.

It's dangerous to encourage a candidate's supporters to write letters to the editor to their local newspaper and then not provide guidance on what to say. A campaign needs to have anything that appears in print to be "on message". The Publicity Coordinator can help supporters write letters by providing some "bullet points" on key matters that the campaign wants to get across in letters to the editor.

Many campaigns provide "suggested" letters to supporters to send in. If you go that route, be sure that the sender is only using the suggested letter as guidance and agrees to put the general contents of the suggested letter into his or her own words. That's important for two reasons: a) newspaper editors will spot "manufactured" letters and not use them and b) its more effective if a local citizen expresses his or her commitment about a candidate or for the candidate's viewpoint if there is a sense that such a letter "came from the heart."

A campaign should encourage people to send in letters to the editor but don't use a "shotgun approach". Your Publicity Coordinator should carefully select, and approach respected and well-liked citizens of the community to write letters to the editor. A letter from a supporter who is a convicted felon or who represents a fringe political group or who is under investigation for embezzlement of funds from a local Girl Scout troop can do more harm than good.

> *Encourage supporters to write letters to the editor but give them some suggestions on content.*

Free Radio Exposure

Free name recognition and issue dissemination from a campaign can effectively be accomplished through radio stations by: a) personal interviews and talk shows, b) news releases and c) commentaries supplied by the candidate.

Radio stations, particularly those in rural districts, will want to have candidate comments to air during news programs. In more urban districts radio stations will be more selective because of the number of political races that need to be covered. Here are some techniques in getting free publicity on radio:

- As a candidate, you should regularly call local stations and ask the news directors if they want a comment from you on a recent news release or issue that is brewing. My experience has been that a news director will usually want to record something while they have a candidate on the phone.

- Before doing a live or taped interview, a candidate would be wise to try and anticipate what a reporter might be asking him to comment about. The candidate should carefully think through what a good response to a question might be.

- When a candidate talks with radio station personnel, he or she should always give them contact information. In more rural areas, the news director may also be an "on air" reporter or personality or otherwise tied to the station, necessitating phone interviews. You want to be easily accessible. You might be surprised how many times a radio station will contact a candidate. It's a good idea for a candidate to carry a folder of all news releases with him. There is nothing worse for a candidate than to be caught saying something on tape that doesn't agree in content with a release that was just sent out.

- As with the print media, news releases sent to radio stations should be short and to the point. Expect broadcasters to read only a portion of a news release over the air. If a candidate's release gets more than 30 seconds of "airtime" during the noon news he or she is doing well.

- Radio talk shows are a great way for a candidate to get name recognition and expose the public to his or her platform. Early in the campaign the Publicity Coordinator should contact every radio station that covers the election district and ascertain if they have a radio talk show. Often such programs are of a "call-in" nature. If they are of that format, the candidate should enlist supporters to call in "planted," friendly, questions. A candidate should anticipate that supporters of the opponent will be calling in unfriendly questions.

> *A candidate should use every opportunity to get coverage through radio interviews.*

- The Publicity Coordinator (or other designated person) can ask the candidate questions in a taped interview and then send the recording to radio stations over the phone or by delivery. Make sure that the answers to questions stay within about 30 seconds. Another technique that is effective is for the campaign to record a candidate's comments before a live audience and then send a short portion to radio stations.

Social Networking Sites

Make use of the Internet! There are many free sites that your Publicity Coordinator can manage that will reach the "connected" crowd. YouTube™, LinkedIn™, Twitter™ and Facebook™ are just a few of the contemporary sites that you can use to get your message across without costing your campaign anything except some time.

This is also an excellent place to put your foot in your mouth. In a recent California election, a candidate was discredited by an opponent who dug up embarrassing social networking posts that the candidate had made several years before. If there's a chance you have a "colorful" history documented online, it is best to be able to justify your statements and recorded activities. While some online activity can be deleted, much cannot and will likely resurface no matter how hard a campaign tries to prevent it. It is much better to be aware and address the risks to your campaign early than to have potentially damaging content, statements, or pictures surface the week before the General Election.

> *Online social networking sites are generally free and reach the "connected" voter. Address any "colorful" online history early in the campaign to prevent it from surfacing at an inopportune time.*

TV Interviews

Unless a campaign is a major race or a high-profile contest, most TV stations will give little coverage to most local political races. A candidate shouldn't be offended. Most TV stations cover large geographical areas and cover several political campaigns simultaneously.

Having said that, a small campaign should keep sending news releases to TV stations and making offers to do interviews with local TV reporters. A TV station may only do one short report on a local race, but because a TV audience is large that could be important.

As with radio interviews, a candidate should anticipate likely questions from TV reporters and think through or practice potential responses. With TV interviews, however, there is an additional element---visual appearance. If called upon to do a TV interview the candidate must make sure that his or her physical appearance is appropriate for the setting. More formal clothing for a sit-down interview is appropriate but wearing formal attire for an interview at a factory or hog farm may look out of place.

Don't forget about local cable TV companies! A candidate should stop in for a short interview or appear on a morning talk program.

> *TV stations seldom cover local races or small campaigns. Nevertheless, a campaign should continually send releases to TV stations and be available for interviews.*

Staying On Message

Candidates will find aggressive reporters in any media. Some reporters will try to trick a candidate into saying something that will get that person in trouble with voters or to say something that will create controversy. Many reporters or editors also have political biases.

A candidate needs to concentrate on "keeping on message". For example:

> Reporter: "As you know, Mrs. Corncob, your opponent has accused you of being soft on environmental protection. How do you respond to that accusation?"
>
> Mrs. Corncob: "My worthy opponent has made a number of unfair and untrue accusations in this campaign. I am NOT soft on the environment. I believe that environmental protection should be based on sound science."
>
> Reporter: "Yes, but you have not spoken out about the Birdfeeder company dumping kryptonite into the Winding River."
>
> Mrs. Corncob: "My opponent reacts emotionally to environmental issues. I will base my decisions on environmental protection based on sound science, not emotion."
>
> Reporter: "Mrs. Corncob, do you know from the scientific evidence that kryptonite causes deformities in earthworms?"
>
> Mrs. Corncob: "Some scientists dispute that. I will study the scientific evidence and make

any decisions on a scientific basis. I am not about to see the loss of 250 jobs at Birdfeeder based on environmental extremism, not scientific fact."

Of course, this is a simplified and fictitious interview, but what did Mrs. Corncob accomplish? She stayed on message (decisions on scientific evidence). She took a dig at her opponent (reacts with emotion instead of scientific evidence). She insinuated that her opponent was an extremist (no decisions on extremism). She is interested in protecting jobs as well as environmental protection (defends jobs over environmental extremism that is not scientifically proven).

The old rule in politics is to "stay on message" no matter what a reporter asks. Before a candidate does any interview with the media, he or she must determine just what that message should be. An aggressive reporter might try to trip up a candidate with some leading questions. A candidate should try to anticipate where that reporter is going before answering any questions.

If a reporter calls a candidate to do an interview, he or she shouldn't be afraid to ask what the subject will be about. That will give the candidate some time to think about the issue and possible answers to anticipated questions. If the candidate knows what the questions will be about and doesn't know the answers, the candidate should simply say that he or she is busy and will call the reporter back.

> *A candidate must "stay on message" no matter how hard a reporter might try to get a candidate to say something the reporter wants.*

Keep Responses Short

When doing an interview, a candidate should concentrate on keeping answers short and to the point. A good reporter may know that an issue is complicated, but the reporter is not the one a candidate is trying to influence. A candidate is trying to influence the voter who will read or hear his comments and may not have a clue of the intricacies of the issue that the candidate is discussing.

Some people criticize politicians for being "evasive" or not having "concrete proposals." That is often not the fault of a person running for office. The truth is that most voters are too busy with their jobs, raising families or doing volunteer work to really study the major, important, issues in a campaign. The best that a candidate can hope for is that a short message will resonate with the voters who really don't have the time for an in-depth explanation of a complicated issue.

> *A candidate needs to keep answers to questions from reporters short and uncomplicated.*

Sarcasms and the Use of Humor

Using humor by telling a short story, joke or reference can often be effective. Care must be taken with the use of humor so that a candidate doesn't come off as not looking serious. Oftentimes self-deprecating humor can be used effectively. A candidate shouldn't be afraid to laugh a little in an interview and make a well-timed funny comment that will get his point across or disarm the opponent.

Maybe the most famous use of humor in recent times occurred during a 1984 Presidential debate between 73 year old President Reagan and his 56 year old challenger Walter Mondale. Reagan knew that his advanced age was an issue in the campaign. At one point in a debate Reagan said age should not be an issue in the campaign and that he would not make an issue out of the "youth and inexperience" of his opponent. ZAP. Issue gone!

Some candidates are comfortable using humor to detract from their opponents or say something funny simply because of the nature of their personality. Most candidates, however, feel somewhat uneasy about using humor in making remarks to the media or before a group. If that is the case, a candidate has two alternatives: a) brainstorm with close associates in coming up with a humorous lines or b) don't try to be humorous but work more on coming across as friendly and approachable. A short laugh about something an opponent said can sometimes go a long way in getting a subliminal message across that the opponent is kidding the voters.

A form of humor is sarcasm, or ridicule. Using sarcasm against an opponent shouldn't be too overt or personal. Use sarcasm without attacking your opponent too directly. Here are some examples:

a) "Ah, my opponent is fibbing again. Why is my opponent hiding his own record?"

b) "My opponent should know better than that. After all, my opponent voted at least fifteen times for tax increases."

c) "I am surprised that my opponent would say that. My opponent claims to be the most knowledgeable candidate in this race. Obviously, that isn't true."

> *Humor and sarcasm are great tools in political campaigns but must be used with caution.*

Chapter 5: General Principles of Campaign Advertising

A campaign must really concentrate on how best to allocate available dollars to most effectively get the candidate's name recognition and message across to the voters. For the purposes of this chapter, we will concentrate on TV, radio, online and print media advertising in general terms. More in-depth discussions will follow in Chapter 6 on print media and Chapter 7 on the electronic media.

What Are the Advantages and Disadvantages of Each Type of Media?

There is really no quick and easy answer to that question. The value of each type of media outlet for political advertising largely depends on the nature of a campaign. If a campaign has lots of money and is a highly visible campaign, more emphasis maybe should be placed on electronic media advertising. If a campaign is in a more rural setting and the race is more localized, print media advertising maybe should be emphasized. Below are some pros and cons of each media type that might help a candidate and his or her Advertising Coordinator in determining budget allocations for paid advertising.

- Television: TV advertising is effective but very expensive. Production costs are high, and a campaign has to run a single ad multiple times in order to be effective. The main problem with TV advertising when running a smaller or local race is that much of a TV station's signal might be going to people who do not live in a candidate's district. If the Election Day for a local candidate's race is the same day of statewide or

Congressional races there is an additional problem: larger campaigns concentrate heavily on TV advertising and the spots for a smaller race will get lost in the mix.

- Radio: A campaign can have the same types of problems with using radio advertising as it does with TV if the race is small, more localized, in an urban setting and there are many other races going on at the same time. A campaign could end up broadcasting ads to a lot of people that can't vote for its candidate and ads might get diluted with ads from many other campaigns. In more rural settings or when running in a geographically large district, however, one or more stations that reach high percentages of the voters that a campaign is trying to reach would be a good investment. An advantage of radio advertising is that it usually is relatively inexpensive. Additionally, radio ads can be produced and on the air much quicker than getting a message to voters through other media- important if there are dynamic issues at the end of a campaign.

- Web Sites and Social Media: The increased availability and affordability of online messaging and advertising cannot be overlooked. In this "new electronic age" creating and maintaining a campaign web page and using social media platforms is a relatively easy way to reach voters, potential supporters and even raise money for the campaign. If you are technologically challenged, have a friend or supporter put together a web page for you and maintain a constant information flow through social media platforms like Facebook. Some online platforms can even be "boosted" or targeted to reach only the people living in a specific area of your district or community.

- Daily Newspapers: The daily newspaper is still important in many political campaigns. It is a little more difficult to determine the "reach" of daily newspapers because they often lay around restaurants, coffee shops, factory lounges, and offices where they are viewed by multiple readers. As is the case with the use of TV and radio advertising, the importance of a particular daily newspaper depends on the ratio of how many of a candidate's voters the paper reaches versus non-voters. Advertising heavily in the Atlanta Constitution for a city council seat in an Atlanta, Georgia, suburb doesn't make much sense. Advertising heavily for a school board seat in Oshkosh, Wisconsin, in the Oshkosh Northwestern that blankets the entire City of Oshkosh makes a great deal of sense. Depending on the cost and the reach of a daily newspaper, a campaign might want to couple its advertising in the printed version with their online internet edition that many dailies now operate.

- Weekly Newspapers: Weekly newspapers are not too prevalent in large, urban areas, but are heavily read in smaller or more rural communities. These local community newspapers cover local weddings, community events, obituaries, neighborhood festivals, local Eagle Scout winners, blue ribbon recipients at the county fair, and other news of local interest. They are read from front to back by "little old ladies." Those little old ladies vote! If a political race is in a more rural constituency with one or more local weekly newspapers, a campaign should consider advertising heavily in this media platform. The cost is relatively low and the reach to potential voters is often great.

- Shoppers: Shoppers have become almost ubiquitous in both rural and urban settings in much of the nation. Their column inch cost is usually very low. Because this media platform is basically page after page of advertising, a campaign's ad can get lost in all the clutter unless it is large or extraordinarily interesting. Many shoppers cover large areas and often print and distribute regional editions of their publications. A campaign would be wise to ascertain if they have more localized editions which will reach the most people a campaign is trying to influence.

- Newsletters: Many neighborhood associations, area business and professional groups, unions and social and fraternal organizations have newsletters that are sent out to their members or residents. Many newsletters sell advertising space. In rural areas the newsletters of farm organizations might reach voters that a campaign might have trouble connecting with. Don't forget church bulletins. Many congregations won't print political advertising but it's worth a few calls to church offices. The big advantage of advertising in newsletters is that a campaign is targeting a select group at a minimal cost.

- Cable TV: Many local cable companies have their own local programming. If they accept advertising, it's generally very inexpensive. Unless a campaign budget is extremely tight, a few dollars invested in this media might be worthwhile.

> *The type of media used in political advertising largely depends on the nature of a race and the "reach" of each media outlet.*

Determining Advertising Value

The value of each media outlet to a campaign basically boils down to how many voters will see or hear the candidate's ad for each dollar spent. Determining the costs per voter reached and putting together an advertising budget will be discussed in the next chapter. Early in a campaign the candidate and his or her Advertising Coordinator need to ascertain which media outlets to advertise in based on some fundamental criteria:

- How many voters in the election district will be reached by each media outlet? Each outlet should be asked to provide to the campaign information on their "reach" into the election district in which the race is being conducted.

- If funds are limited, a campaign has to concentrate especially hard in maximizing the impact of each dollar spent. Limited financial resources will force a campaign to advertise only with those outlets which reach the most voters at the lowest cost. If a campaign is financially strong it can afford to advertise in media outlets that otherwise might be considered marginal.

- Are there media outlets that a campaign could be spending a lot of money on primarily reaching non-voters? It doesn't make much sense to buy expensive TV advertising if the market of a TV station is 5% in a candidate's election district and 95% outside the election district, even if its reach is 100% within the election district.

- Are there media outlets that may not reach many potential voters, but are so inexpensive that a campaign shouldn't resist? Some local cable companies, for example, have local programming that is not viewed by many people but offer advertising that costs only pocket change.

- What combination of media should a campaign use? To reach as many voters as possible, a campaign needs to invest paid advertising dollars in a variety of media outlets. A radio station might reach 60% of targeted voters on a daily basis. Advertising through that station might be smart, but what about the other 40% of voters? What media outlets do they turn to for news, community information and entertainment?

> *The value of each media outlet to a campaign is sometimes influenced by factors other than simply the cost/voter reached.*

Timing is Everything

OK, it's getting close to the election, your spouse hasn't seen you in months, your kids call the police when you eventually come home thinking that you are a burglar, and your dog bites you at the door. Welcome to the world of intensive campaigning (and you thought that democracy and winning an election would be easy).

One of the biggest mistakes that campaigns make is getting in a panic mode in a tough race and spending too much on advertising too early. If you don't take in anything else from reading this book, remember this: MOST VOTERS ARE NOT PAYING ATTENTION TO THE ELECTION UNTIL THE LAST TEN DAYS.

That doesn't mean that a candidate should wait until the last ten days to go door-to-door, attend coffees and hold fundraising events. It simply means that in planning advertising (a huge chunk of a campaign's total budget), a campaign needs to concentrate on the last weeks before the election.

Generally, a campaign shouldn't start running media advertising prior to four weeks before the election. There are four exceptions to that rule:

a) Advertise fundraising events that the campaign wants people to attend. If the Governor is speaking at a sit-down dinner for the candidate, advertise the event. If the campaign is holding a spaghetti feed at the local veterans' hall, advertise the event.

b) Advertise meet-the-candidate events such as a booth at the county fair or a listening session at the local village hall. Such ads don't communicate issues, but they do send a message that a candidate wants to meet the voters and listen to their concerns.

c) Advertise to solicit volunteers and funds. A campaign might want to run a few ads to solicit campaign funds and volunteers early in the race. A simple ad might contain a coupon that voters can send in or an email address for volunteering. Experience has proven that such solicitations don't raise a lot of money or sign up a lot of workers. Don't worry. The main focus isn't to accomplish those goals anyway. The focus is to show voters that they are welcomed to join the campaign.

d) Do specialty ads if the campaign anticipates a lot of absentee voters or voting is allowed early in non-traditional balloting like mail-in voting.

> *Most political advertising should wait until the last 4 weeks before Election Day.*

Remember to KISS

No, I am not referring to kissing babies. K.I.S.S. stands for "Keep It Simple, Stupid". Many candidates, especially rookies, think that they are going to educate the voters on the issues and make them all very appreciative of the civics lessons dished out by the office-seeker. Surely the voters will be impressed with a candidate's detailed explanations of complicated public matters. Some candidates actually believe that the more complicated they get in explaining an issue the more likely that they will be elected. Wrong. They lose.

Oh yes, there are many voters who really pay attention to the issues and ask intelligent questions of candidates. Many of them may know the issues better than the candidates. Those really "educated" voters will seek out definitive answers from candidates. The vast majority of voters, however, do not have the time or the inclination to study the issues in-depth and be persuaded by an intelligent discourse with a candidate. It's time for K.I.S.S.

"Keep It Simple, Stupid" is simply a reminder to a campaign that it cannot get its message too complicated. Remember that a campaign has to market a candidate and what he or she stands for to the average voter. Through paid advertising, a campaign must use simple sound bites and easy-to-read ads to reach average voters. If a campaign gets too complicated and "wordy" in ads it will lose the interest of the voters it is trying to reach.

Political ads must be short and simple.

Getting Too Complicated: A Story on the K.I.S.S. of Death

Get too complicated and you are sure to lose your election. Keep in mind K.I.S.S (Keep It Simple, Stupid). As a candidate, you have to sell the voters on yourself and the issues you are running on in your platform. Most voters care about elections but are just too busy to spend a lot of time doing an in-depth analysis of the issues for each candidate. That's where a candidate and campaign advertising come in.

Recommendations on some specific tactics and principles of political advertising will be discussed in the next two chapters. For now, I just want to relate to you a real instance of how a candidate can lose an election by getting his or her message too complicated (forgetting K.I.S.S.).

During one general election I was an incumbent State Senator and in the middle of a four-year term. I was asked by party leaders to advise a candidate running for State Representative since I was interested in the race, there was a strong belief that my party's candidate would win, and I had the time to help.

Frank (not his real name) was a popular mayor of the largest city in his legislative district. When he announced his candidacy, he had broad support from members of both major political parties and a lot of independents. Getting people to donate to his campaign was not a problem. In fact, Frank's campaign treasury was awash in cash. Frank's incumbent opponent was mistrusted by many voters and had voted against the interests of the district on numerous occasions.

Most people felt that Frank would win the election. There

was only one problem with Frank. He didn't take advice very well from people who knew better than he did about how to win an election.

Early in the campaign I met with Frank and his campaign committee. We all agreed on how the campaign would be organized, what the issues should be and how the campaign should be executed. We even went over a tentative media advertising budget.

I called or met with Frank on a regular basis. It seemed that he was doing all the right things. He was knocking on doors, attending community events, doing media interviews and giving talks before local organizations.

Three weeks before the election I called Frank and told him that I was concerned that I hadn't seen any ads for his candidacy in the local media. "Oh, don't worry," he said. "I have a secret plan."

Then two weeks before the election I called Frank again. "Frank, what are you doing with all that money we raised for your campaign? I haven't seen one ad in a newspaper or heard one ad over radio for your campaign."

"Oh, don't worry. I have a secret plan," he assured me again.

I wasn't assured. I was getting downright nervous about what this secret plan was of Frank. I told Frank that he and his committee needed to make its print and electronic media campaign purchases soon while the interest in the campaign was nearing a peak.

A week before the election... "Hey, Frank, where are the ads for your campaign? You have plenty of money in your campaign account to do a great job in advertising. You just have to get those ads going now. Do you want me to write them?"

"No, I am fine. As I told you, I have a secret plan. You are going to love it."

On Election Day I found out what Frank's secret plan was. I opened the morning daily newspaper that covered most of Frank's district. I sat back in horror. There it was in 50,000 words: full page after full page of Frank's views on every major issue in the campaign.

Frank called and asked me what I thought about his secret plan. "Frank, you lose," I said with remorse. "Not even your mother would read all your comments before going to the polls today."

Frank lost. No, I should say that Frank was ground into the pavement in a race that he should have won. He wouldn't follow my advice in keeping his message simple and he paid dearly for it. He forgot K.I.S.S.

Active and Positive Lead Words

When putting together political ads an Advertising Coordinator should concentrate on the use of verbs that evoke toughness, action and passion. Words like "fight for", "demand", "insist" and "strongly support" will always trump lead words like "vote for", "push for" and plain old "support". "Alice Pinetree will <u>fight for</u> better environmental protection" sounds more passionate and committed than "Alice Pinetree <u>supports</u> better environmental protection."

Voters often say that they know what individual politicians are AGAINST but don't know what they are FOR. Play into that; use a candidate's positions on what he is FOR more than what he is AGAINST. For example, it's better to say that "Jason Pinhead will fight <u>for</u> more efficient county government" rather than "Jason Pinhead is <u>against</u> inefficient county government". Usually, campaign ads should put a positive spin on things and subliminally send a message to the voters that a candidate stands FOR issues that matter to the people. A little bit of positive thinking goes a long way.

> *Use active and positive words in ads to send a message.*

Do Ads Grab Attention and Make Sense?

Before shipping ads out to media outlets, a candidate and his or her Advertising Coordinator should invite some friends over and ask them to be brutally honest in critiquing proposed campaign ads. An Advertising Coordinator might want to produce more ads than are intended to be used so that some of the attendees can have input in the final selections. The campaign should use "rough drafts" at this stage to garner opinions before final versions are made.

Does each ad make logical sense? I once read an ad by a candidate that questioned why an incumbent legislator voted for and against certain bills and listed only the bill numbers, not the issues in the bills. "Did you know that Representative Smith voted against House Bill 382?" OK, what does that mean? Is that the bill to designate National Trash Haulers Day or the one to legalize gambling and prostitution?

If an ad is not logical and does not evoke a clear message, caution should be used. If a candidate's supporters don't understand an ad, average Joe citizen certainly won't know why a campaign spent good money for the ad.

> *Do proposed ads make sense? Do they get the proper message across and attract interest? Some of the candidate's supporters should have input.*

Don't Forget Legal Requirements

In most jurisdictions all political media advertising-print and electronic-will require a disclaimer (the Authorized and Paid For By...). For radio advertising either the ad or the disclaimer must also contain the voice of the candidate.

I always tell candidates to "attack the issues, not the person." At all costs, a candidate should avoid defaming his or her opponent with the intent of injuring the character or reputation of that individual with inaccurate statements. Making false statements about an individual can result in a lawsuit for libel (written false statement) or slander (spoken false statement). Any candidate that engages in personal character assassination with false accusations is likely to see his or her attack backfire.

> *Pay attention to legal requirement and avoid potential legal problems.*

Always Be Accurate and Honest

A campaign must make sure that the information provided in an ad is accurate and can be substantiated. That is particularly true if a candidate is doing an attack ad against his opponent. If a candidate makes outright false statements about an opponent's stance or record on the issues he or she should expect to be hauled in before election officials and greatly increase the likelihood that he or she will lose the election. If election officials don't question the accuracy of a candidate's charges, you can bet that the media will. Let me give you an example from personal experience.

In my second re-election campaign for my state legislative seat I was running scared. My opponent was well-known throughout the district and was a member of the city council in the largest city in the district (I lived in the second largest city). My opponent was also on the National Committee of her political party. My opponent had the Governor, the area Congressman and a popular United States Senator campaigning against me in my district. Things looked pretty dismal.

Then it happened! Right before the election my opponent ran a large ad in newspapers stating that I had voted AGAINST three issues that would have been popular in my district to support. The truth was I voted in FAVOR of all three issues. The charges in the ad of my opponent were complete fabrications.

The next day my campaign ran a large ad in response. We simply provided evidence from the official legislative records that showed that I had voted in favor of the three bills my opponent said that I had voted against.

I won the election by a landslide. I even won 2-1 in the hometown and in the city council ward of my opponent.

> *Always be accurate and honest in ads or you will be in trouble.*

Don't Forget About Deadlines

A campaign can make up the best ads in the world but if they do not get to the media by a deadline for getting broadcast or printed it's all for nothing. Many radio stations, for example, require recorded ads to be in the possession of a station three days before they are to air along with written transcripts of each ad. A daily newspaper may require a two or three day lead time for printing political ads. Weekly newspapers and shoppers that might be delivered on a Thursday or Friday often have a deadline to receive ads by the preceding Friday.

The Advertising Coordinator has to know those deadlines and to adhere to them. Importantly, the Advertising Coordinator must give some lead time to the Treasurer to be able to write checks for the ads before the ads are delivered.

> ***Pay attention to media outlet deadlines and get ads in on time.***

Chapter 6: Media Advertising Budgets and Ad Types

A candidate cannot expect to win a political campaign without having a well-organized and well- financed advertising budget. Since a campaign reaches more voters through advertising than any other campaign activity, how much that is spent and where it is spent becomes very important.

Making an Advertising Budget

Early in a campaign it's difficult to know exactly what funds will be available in the crucial final days of the campaign to pay for media advertising. For most campaigns its best to work off a conservative media advertising budget. If the financial situation of a campaign turns out better than expected, the campaign can always throw in more ads with the electronic media and bigger ads in the print media in the final days of the campaign.

For purposes of example, let's say that a candidate is running in a race for a local office and expects to have $15,000 in campaign funds to spend on paid media advertising. Let's also assume that the election district has 20,000 voters. The candidate and the Advertising Coordinator should put together a budget of how much is going to be allocated to each media outlet.

The Advertising Coordinator should start by finding out the percentage of households in the election district that receive advertising from each media outlet (the outlet's "reach"). Then the Advertising Coordinator should put down the cost of a "unit" of advertising: 30 second spot for the electronic media and the cost per column inch for the print media. The Advertising Coordinator should then determine the cost per voter reached for each media outlet: the number of voters times the "reach" of the media outlet equals the number of voters reached. The cost per unit divided by the number of voters reached equals the cost per voter through a given media outlet.

Example: The Hometown Daily reaches 96% of the voters in the district and costs $12/column inch. 20,000 x 0.96 = 19,200 voters reached. $12 divided by 19,200 = 0.006 cost per voter reached.

Media Outlet	"Reach" In District	Cost Per Unit	Cost Per Voter Reached	Suggested Budget
Channel 2 TV	100%	$545/ 30 sec. ad	$0.0273	$0
Radio Station VVVV	20%	$38/ 30 sec. ad	$0.0095	$500
Radio Station ABCD	80%	$72/ 30 sec. ad	$0.0045	$2,500
Hometown Daily	96%	$12/ col-inch	$0.0006	$8,000
Main Street Shopper	20%	$4/ col-inch	$0.0010	$750
People's Weekly	10%	$8.50/ col-inch	$0.0043	$250
Tri-City Tabloid	60%	$10/ col-inch	$0.0008	$3,000

In this example the least costly outlet for each voter reached is the Hometown Daily and the most expensive is Channel 2 TV. A campaign certainly wants to devote a large chunk of the paid media advertising budget to the Hometown Daily. Although Channel 2 TV covers the entire district, it is expensive. A campaign might want to advertise on Channel 2 only if the campaign is awash with more cash than originally anticipated.

While a campaign needs to concentrate available advertising dollars where it can get the "most bang for the buck", a campaign shouldn't entirely neglect the outlets that are more expensive per voter reached. Radio station ABCD is a lot less expensive per voter reached than Station VVVV. An Advertising Coordinator certainly would want to concentrate electronic media buys on ABCD, but he or she should consider a smaller buy toward the end of the campaign on Station VVVV. Similarly, the Tri-City Tabloid looks like a good bargain, but the campaign may want to include a few ads in the Main Street Shopper and the People's Weekly.

> *Start the budget process by determining the cost per voter reached.*

Print Media Advertising Budget

After determining an overall budget allocation for each media outlet for the campaign, it's now time to determine the size of the ads each week and how much you intend to spend. A weekly "buy" budget might look like this:

Media*	Budget	$/col-In	Week 4	Week 3	Week 2	Week 1
Hometown Daily**	$8k	$12	$432	$864	$1,404	$5,312
Tri-City Tabloid***	$3k	$10	3x7 ($210)	3x7 ($210), 3x10 ($300)	4x17 ($680)	6x18 Front Page ($1,620)
Main Street Shopper	$750	$4	3x7 ($84)	3x10 ($120)	(2) 3x7 ($168)	4x17 ($272), 3x7 ($84)
People's Weekly	$250	$8.50			2x5 ($85)	3x7 ($178.50)

*Assume that all papers are 6 columns by 21 inches, for purposes of example. Ads are sold by the "column inch" which is the width of a column times the height of an ad in inches.

**See detailed budget for the Hometown Daily is below.

*** Assumes that the advertising space on the front page of the Tri-City Tabloid is 108 column inches (minus the heading at the top) and that the cost is $15/column inch instead of the usual $10/ column inch.

Notice that we start with small ads four weeks before the election and build up the number of column inches every week. As stated earlier, a campaign should always "budget backwards". If money is short, a campaign should cut the number of column inches planned to be purchased in week four, not in the week before the election. Budgeting for advertising sometimes gets to be a guessing game because donations to political campaigns often increase significantly as an election approaches. That is particularly true for the candidate who appears to be winning the race.

Notice that we didn't precisely stay within the budget. We budgeted $250 for the People's Weekly, for example, but will be spending $263.50. We budgeted $750 for the Main Street Shopper and will be spending $728. The overall media budget can just be rounded off to make it easy to understand. The important thing is to purchase the number of column inches close to your print media budget.

> Build up the weekly number of column inches as Election Day approaches.

Daily Newspaper Budget

Three of the publications in our example come out on a weekly basis so showing the sizes of ads on a weekly basis is not a problem in the budget above. For a daily publication like the Hometown Daily, a campaign needs to budget for each day of the week for the four weeks preceding the election:

An advertising budget for the Hometown Daily might look something like this:

> Daily newspaper "buys" must be budgeted on a day-by-day basis.

Day Before Election*	Size And Number Of Ads	Cost
Election Day, Tues.	Front Page Box ($500), 6x9 ($648)	$1,148
1, Mon.	4x17 ($816), 6x9 ($648)	$1,464
2, Sun.**	3x10 (360)	$360
3, Sat.	3x10 ($360), 3x7 ($252)	$612
4, Fri.	3x16 ($576)	$576
5, Thu.	6x9 ($648)	$648
6, Wed.	3x14 ($504)	$504
7, Tu.	3x7 ($252)	$252
8, Mon.	3x7 ($252)	$252
9, Sun.	-0-	-0-
10, Sat.	3x7 ($252)	$252
11, Fri.	3x7 ($252)	$252
12, Thu.	3x7 ($252)	$252
13, Wed.	2x6 ($144)	$144
14, Tu.	2x6 ($144)	$144
15, Mon.	2x6 ($144)	$144
16, Sun.	-0-	-0-
17, Sat.	2x6 ($144)	$144
18, Fri.	2x6 ($144)	$144
19, Thu.	2x6 (144)	$144
20, Wed.	2x6 ($144)	$144
21, Tu.	2x4 ($96)	$96
22, Mon.	2x4 ($96)	$96
23, Sun.	-0-	-0-
24, Sat.	2x4 ($96)	$96
25, Fri.	2x2 ($48)	$48
26, Thu.	2x2 ($48)	$48
27, Wed.	2x2 ($48)	$48

*A weekly budget for a daily newspaper should be Tuesday back to the preceding Wednesday, assuming that Election Day is on a Tuesday.

**Don't advertise on Sundays except the last Sunday before the election. Sunday daily papers are so full of ads that any ad a campaign buys may get lost.

Electronic Media Advertising Budget

As with the print media, a campaign needs to determine how much it will spend each week with electronic media. In our example from the budget above, an electronic media "buy" might look like this:

Media	Budget	Cost/30 Sec. Spot	Week 4	Week 3	Week 2	Week 1
Chan. 2 TV	-0-	$545	-0-	-0-	-0-	-0-
Radio Sta. VVVV	$500	$38	-0-	-0-	5 ads $190	8 ads $304
Radio Sta. ABCD	$2,500	$72	5 ads $360	5 ads $360	8 ads $576	16 ads $1,152

Below are some cautions about advertising in the electronic media for a small campaign:

- Budgeting for radio ads is tricky. Advertising in the print media is generally not impacted by time of day considerations. A daily newspaper with a candidate's ad may arrive in the morning and be seen throughout the day by several individuals in a household or at a workplace. Getting the attention of voters through radio ads is different. More people will hear an ad during peak drive times and during popular daytime programs than at other times of the day. A campaign likely will have to pay a premium to get its ads to air during those prime times.

- TV advertising is financially prohibitive for many smaller campaigns but is more important for races for higher office. TV advertising reaches a broad audience, but it is expensive. A candidate could end up bringing his or her message to many people who are not the voters in the targeted district. Unless a campaign is extremely well financed, I recommend that candidates in smaller campaigns forget about TV advertising. If TV is to be used, a campaign needs to consider whether it can afford placing ads in the prime-time evening hours.

- Radio and TV ads are most effective if they saturate the airwaves before an election. People tend to "tune off" political ads on radio and TV. When advertising in the electronic media it's best to buy lots of ads and have those ads run largely in peak times when the most voters are tuned in.

- Many electronic media outlets will offer promotions to sell ads during non-peak times that are so inexpensive that they are hard to pass up. Before considering buying those ads, a campaign should find out from the outlet what the audience rating (the "reach") is during those non-peak times in the district or community being targeted. After finding out that information, a campaign should determine the cost per voter reached (number of voters x "reach" divided into the cost for a 30 second ad). It might be that the cost for ads during non-peak times is so inexpensive that a campaign might want to buy a package of them.

- As mentioned before, advertising during "local access" programs on cable TV are generally inexpensive but may not reach too many voters. A campaign might want to throw a few dollars into this media, but it shouldn't go overboard.

> *Try scheduling electronic media ads during times when the most voters are tuned in.*

The Types of Ads

There are basically six different types of political ads- printed or electronic-and each one is intended to convey a different message to the voter or to enlist different responses:

a) The Image Ad.
Image ads should be designed to tell voters with pictures and a few words that a candidate is a nice, trustworthy, likable person. If a candidate's looks and personality don't relate well with the voters, it doesn't matter much what the issues are, that candidate is going to have a tough time getting elected.

Remember the old saying that "a picture is worth a thousand words." That saying certainly is true when an Advertising Coordinator is making up an image ad. Most image ads devote little space to issues and then only in general terms. They do, however, have a flattering picture of the candidate meeting voters or a family photo.

b) The Endorsement Ad.
Endorsement ads can be very effective. They convey to voters the notion that a lot of other people and groups support a candidate. They can be tricky, however. A campaign needs to be careful in using the names of individuals or organizations that support a candidate since some might not be all that popular in the election district. For example, a candidate wouldn't want to have the endorsement of a convicted pedophile or bank robber. A candidate wouldn't want to tell people in a conservative community that he or she has the backing of a radical fringe group or militant labor union.

When considering running an endorsement ad, a campaign is much better off running an ad with the names of people supporting its candidate than organizations providing endorsements. Having community leaders publicly stating their support for a candidate has more impact than bragging about the fact that the candidate has support from a special interest group. Many people are suspicious about organizations that endorse candidates but feel more comfortable supporting a candidate that has the open support of prominent individuals in the community. There are exceptions to that advice: if there are groups that are popular or dominate an election district, it's perfectly appropriate to advertise that such groups support the candidate. If a candidate is running in a community where 75% of the voters work in the paper manufacturing industry, it's safe for a candidate to tell voters that he has the support of the local paper workers' union.

The most effective endorsement ad is one in which prominent individuals actually agree to have their signatures included in a print media ad. The headline of the ad might be something like "We support honest government and job development. That's why we support Joe Snowplow for State Senate." That would be followed by columns with the signatures of people who support the candidate. Readers will spend some time seeing who is so committed to the candidate that they would affix their personal signature to a political ad.

c) The Issue Ad.

The issue ad is the staple of political advertising. It tells voters where the candidate stands on the issues. Generally, a campaign doesn't want to include more than six to eight issues in such and ad, and then only in summary fashion (remember K.I.S.S.).

While an Advertising Coordinator should summarize or simplify the issues placed in issue ads, a candidate needs to be prepared to answer questions as to how exactly the issue would be addressed, if asked. Having a campaign ad saying that the candidate is for ethics in government, for example, doesn't answer the question of what he or she would do on that issue if elected. A candidate will look silly if he is at a candidate forum and a voter stands up and asks what the candidate would do to improve ethics in government and he or she doesn't have an answer.

d) The Comparison Ad.
If there are considerable differences between a candidate and his or her opponent it might help to publicize those differences, provided that:

- The candidate can verify the positions of his opponent by statements or votes he or she made.

AND,

- A comparison ad will place the candidate on the side of the majority of voters.

A good comparison ad will have a picture of both the candidate and his or her opponent. If a campaign can acquire an unflattering picture of the opponent, that is all the better. A campaign cannot get too complicated in a comparison ad. It needs to stick with only a few issues that it knows will resonate with the voters. An effective approach is to include a column in the ad where readers can vote (Column 1: the issue; Column 2: the opponent's position; Column 3: your candidate's position, Column 4: a blank for the voter to check-off "for or against" or "yes or no").

e) The Attack Ad.
An attack ad directly attacks the vote record, statements or positions on the issues of the opponent. In doing an

attack ad, an Advertising Coordinator might want to stick with only a few topics. If, for example, the opponent has some known ethical problems, made false or misleading statements or supports issues that are contrary to the majority opinion of the voters, then a campaign should hit those issues hard, but keep it simple.

CAUTION: In attacking an opponent a campaign must make sure that any statements made are accurate and can be documented. Inaccurate statements by a candidate will be counter-attacked viciously by his or her opponent or the media and can doom a campaign. They also can get a candidate into legal problems with violations of election rules and libel and slander lawsuits. A campaign must always double check everything in an attack ad and make sure that any statement cannot be labeled as being a dishonest portrayal of the opponent.

f) The Humorous Ad

The humorous might not convey many issues but it is designed to make voters laugh a little and remember the candidate behind it. Humorous ads can poke fun of the opponent in a playful manner but must not be objectionable. Humorous ads are tricky to produce! A campaign must make sure that the subject of the proposed humor is truly humorous. A good tactic is to invite people not associated with the campaign to hear or read the proposed ad and give their critiques.

Humorous ads in the electronic media often employ recorded "laughing". Don't let that bother you. TV shows often use "canned" laughter to make episodes of programs all the time.

Campaigns should "mix and match" ad types throughout the weeks before the election. Voters don't want to hear just attack ads from a candidate on the radio or just see pretty pictures of the candidate in image ads in the newspaper. A comparison ad might be followed by an image ad which might be followed by an attack ad, for example.

> **An effective campaign will use a variety of ad types to attract voter interest.**

Chapter 7: Print Media Advertising

For smaller campaigns, print media advertising is more likely to be a focal point of advertising than the electronic media. How a campaign utilizes ad buys in the print media could determine the outcome of the race.

Start Small, Grow Big

Remember that most voters are not paying much attention to the upcoming elections until the last ten days. While you have been working six to eight months to build your campaign and meeting voters, the average voter is going to class reunions, taking the kids to piano lessons, doing some gardening and watching sports on TV. It's not that they are un-patriotic; it's just that your campaign is not important to most voters until they actually have to make a decision on whom to vote for.

If most voters are not paying attention to your campaign until the very end, when should you start print media advertising? My advice is that you start four weeks before the election. Start with small ads in the print media just to get your name out and to address a few issues. As was covered in Chapter 6, a campaign should increase ad sizes and the number of ads the week before the election.

> *Start with small ads and grow the size of ads as Election Day approaches.*

Ad Placement is Important

"Placement" of print ads is as important in the print media as is maximizing exposure in the electronic media, depending on the amount of available funds. Is there a local high school football team that is having a winning season and is well covered in the *Hometown Gazette*? Paying a little extra for a guaranteed placement of an ad on the sports page might be wise. Placing a large ad on page 3 is good. Pick up a newspaper. Look at the front page. Then turn the page. Do you first look at page 2 or page 3?

Some daily newspapers (and a few weeklies) sell what is known in the business as the "Front Page Box". It is the only advertisement that is allowed on the front page of a newspaper. It is fairly expensive but worth it. A Front Page Box generally is only a column wide by two to three inches high. You won't be able to educate voters on the issues in such a small space. Just fit in your picture, your name, the office being sought after and your disclaimer.

Early in a campaign consideration should be given to reserving the entire front page of any advertising shopper in the edition that comes out right before Election Day and covers a large number of homes in the district. Such an ad is more expensive than regular random ads in a shopper, but its well worth the extra expense. It will be the first ad that voters see. It may sit around homes and workplaces for days with your smiling face looking up at the voters.

> *Sometimes paying extra to assure ad placement is a wise choice.*

Doing Your Own Paper

I have seen some campaigns do an effective job of printing up their own tabloids. Sometimes these can be made to look just like a newspaper, albeit only a few pages long. Such tabloids can be filled with lots of flattering photos of the candidate and a listing of the candidate's position on the issues. Oftentimes such tabloids are distributed by volunteers to homes right before an election or inserted for nominal costs into a daily or weekly newspaper.

> *A campaign tabloid can be an inexpensive way to reach voters.*

Make Your Ads Look Bigger Than They Are

The rule in print media advertising is "the bigger the better". Print media advertising outside major metropolitan areas is relatively inexpensive. There are so many ads in the print media that your ad will get lost if it is not large in size. However, there are a few tricks to consider in making your ads look large and save your campaign money in the process. Suppose the size of your local newspaper is 11 inches x 21 inches and 6 columns wide (sizes may vary and be as much as 23.5" long). You might want to consider some of the following to save money and have an impact:

a) Placing several 3 columns x 7 inch ads are relatively inexpensive but they really stand out.

b) Instead of buying a full page six columns x 21 inch ad, how about a 4 column x 17 inch or a 3 column x 17 inch ad? You haven't purchased the whole page, but your ad will dominate the page that it is on.

c) A normal half page ad in our example would be 6 columns x 10.5 inches (half of 21 inches). You could purchase an ad that is 6 columns by 9 inches and have about the same visual impact.

d) Some print media allow "banner ads". These are ads that will run across a page but only be a few inches high. Ask about such ads when you are talking to print media advertising people.

e) Newspapers charge by the column inch (one column wide and one inch high). A standard newspaper layout is 6 columns by 21 inches tall. If you order a "3 x 7" ad you're paying for an ad that is 3 columns wide and 7 inches tall. You will be charged for "21 inches." You can order a full week, just weekdays, alternating days or other options. Expect to pay extra for guaranteed ad placement, banner ads and front page box ads.

> *Save money by purchasing ad sizes that look bigger than they really are.*

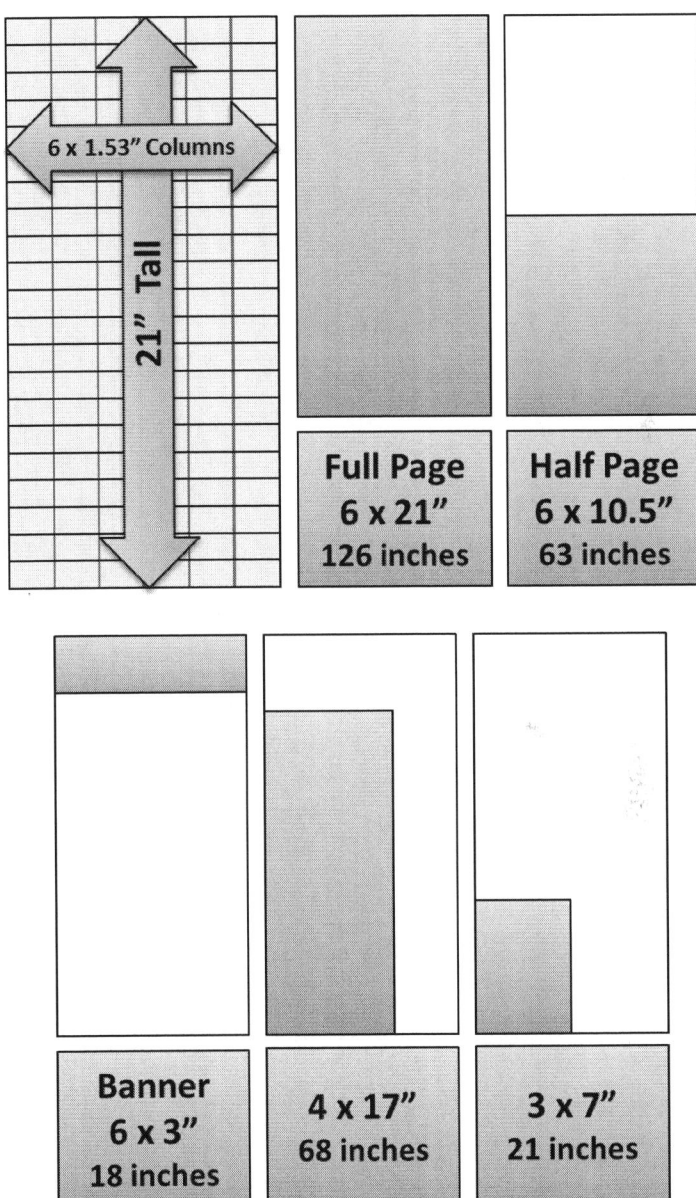

Big Picture/ Big Name/Little Copy

Time yourself. How long in does it take you to thumb through the local newspaper-weekly or daily? Five minutes? Ten minutes? Most people will read through the first few paragraphs of a story that interests them and only take a passing glance at advertisements. Political advertisements generally receive even less eye contact than other forms of advertising.

The important thing to remember in print advertisements for political campaigns is: BIG PICTURE/BIG NAME/little copy:

- Your main picture that you use in most advertising and handouts should be a clear "head shot" (shoulders up). A picture of your family in a relaxing setting is good. An ad appealing to farmers should have a picture of you with a farmer and maybe a cow or tractor in the background. In an ad in a heavily unionized or working-class neighborhood, a pose with some workers next to machinery would be suitable. The important thing is to have a photo in an ad that is appropriate to the interests of the voters you are trying to target.

- Have a friend who knows something about photography take a number of pictures of you on the campaign trail in various meetings with people to be used in print advertising. In smaller campaigns especially, it is important that pictures in print advertising be more informal and "folksy". Wearing a suit and looking like you are addressing the United Nations General Assembly doesn't fit a campaign for city council in a community of 3,000 people.

- If the picture in an ad is just of you, have your face looking toward the copy in the ad (i.e. if your face in a head shot photo is tilted toward the right it should be on the right side of the ad "looking" toward the copy on the left). That will have the tendency of drawing people's attention toward the copy.

- One of the biggest mistakes in smaller campaigns is the notion that people (voters) are going to really know the complexities of the issues. DO NOT try to over-educate the voters (remember K.I.S.S.) in print advertisements! Your campaign can buy a full-page ad in a daily newspaper and explain in 10,000 words or more where you stand on the issues. It won't be read! Remember the true story of "Frank" in the Chapter 5? It is better for you to summarize your issues in a few, succinct, bullet points in an ad. Such an ad will at least get a few seconds of attention by a voter which is your goal in the first place.

- Your name, your picture and the office you are running for should be very prominent in a print media ad. These three parts of the ad should take up at least half the ad space.

- Leave lots of white space! After you have selected your appropriate photo and the copy for your ad, be sure to arrange your ad so that that there is lots of "white space" left. Test this out on yourself; look over a newspaper and think about the ads that your eyes are attracted to and that you read. I bet they are the ads with a large photo and little copy (verbiage). Go through the paper quickly. Do you remember any of the ads with lots of copy (verbiage)? Point made.

Simple Ad:

WE NEED A STRONG VOICE IN WESTMINSTER!

Henry Alarmclock will:

- Fight for better funding of schools

- Strongly support property tax relief

- Demand more efficient state government

- Push hard for better roads in our end of the state

- Fight for campaign finance reform

- Insist on ethics in government

ELECT

ALARMCLOCK

State Senator
"A Strong Voice In Westminster"
(disclaimer)

Complicated Ad:

WE NEED A STRONG VOICE IN WESTMINSTER!
Henry Alarmclock will fight for:

- Better funding for our schools. He believes that the state school aid formula is flawed, and that more emphasis must be placed on providing more money to schools in low income areas. He also believes in state financial assistance for updating school facilities.
- Harry Alarmclock believes that increased state aid for education coupled with caps on spending increases by schools and local governments will reduce the burden of property taxes on our citizens. Harry also supports a freeze in property taxes for lower income senior citizens and assessing farmlands based on use rather than market value.
- Harry Alarmclock will work toward making state government more efficient by reducing paperwork, moving toward a "zero budgeting" system, increase computer backlogs in the Department of Justice and setting up fiscal accountability boards for each department.
- Better highways in our region of the state will be a priority once Harry Alarmclock is elected. He will work to get a seat on the Transportation Commission. He will support a change in the formula for allocating highway funds solely on traffic counts and too much money going into mass transit rather than roads.
- Harry Alarmclock supports caps on donations to political candidates and total spending by candidates. He believes that too much money is spent on campaigns and that its time to reduce the influence of money in campaigns.

ALARMCLOCK
State Senator
"A Strong Voice In Westminster"
(disclaimer)

What ad are you more likely to glance at or actually read? Having lots of "white space" and only a little copy is the most effective approach. The key is to not bore the reader (voter) with too many words.

> **Print ads should have BIG picture, BIG name, and little copy.**

How Many Issues Should a Candidate Cover in a Print Media Ad?

Very few! Remember Big Picture/ Big Name/Little Copy. Also remember K.I.S.S.

First of all, you and your Advertising Coordinator have to determine if a particular ad is meant to be an "image ad," an "endorsement ad," an "issue ad," a "comparison ad," a "humorous ad" or an "attack ad":

a) Generally, few real campaign issues are mentioned in an image ad. In an image ad you are only trying to convey the notion that you are a nice, likable, trustworthy, friendly person.

b) An endorsement ad conveys to voters that a lot of other people support your candidacy. Instead of hard-hitting issues and endorsement ad is more likely to say something like "We support Sally Small for Council because she knows the issues and listens to the people..." followed by the names of people supporting the candidacy.

c) An issue ad should tell voters where you stand on the issues. Don't go beyond 6-8 topics in an issue ad and only then in summary form.

d) A humorous ad generally should not have more than 2-3 issues or matters being poked fun of. Many times, it is just one statement or position of the opponent that you are trying to get people laughing at.

e) A comparison ad is a variation of the "issue ad" and should convey the difference between you and your opponent on the issues. Again, restrict the number of issues to no more than six to eight.

f) An attack ad questions the votes, statements or positions on the issues of the opponent. To be most effective, an attack ad should be restricted to only a few issues.

> *The number of issues in an ad should be kept to a minimum.*

Examples of the Types of Print Media Ads

In the last chapter you learned that there are six basic types of ads-Issue, Endorsement, Image, Humorous, Comparison and Attack. Here are some examples of each type of ad:

a) Issue ads communicate to voters where you stand on some issues. Remember K.I.S.S.

Mary Pinecone is a worker! Here's what she will work for as a member of the City Council:

- Expanded job opportunities
- More open government
- Street improvements
- Better park maintenance
- Honesty in government

ELECT
MARY PINECONE
City Council-District 9
"Because We Deserve Her"
(disclaimer)

---

b) Endorsement ads need to be used with caution. Remember, some individuals or organizations might not be popular with everyone in your community.

We believe that Joe Piecrust is the best candidate for County Commissioner.

Chris Crescent   Charlie Casserole
Betty Breadbox   Bill Bundt
Danny Doughnuthole   Lucy Layercake
Percy Popover   Mary Muffinmix
Sam Scone   Bert Browniesquares

---Re-Elect---

PIECRUST

County Commissioner

(disclaimer)

c) Comparison ads are designed to show the differences between you and your opponent. Be sure that you can back up the differences with documentation.

Before you vote, compare the candidates for District Attorney:

ISSUE	Sally Onion	John Squash	YOUR vote
Supports expanded use of school drug liaison officers	YES	NO	
Will fight to eliminate backlog of court cases	YES	NO	
Supports keeping the drinking age at 21	YES	NO	
Favors determinant sentencing	YES	NO	
Wants upgrades in security at the county jail	YES	NO	

Sally Onion is on <u>YOUR</u> side!

ELECT
ONION
DISTRICT ATTORNEY
"The Better Choice"
(disclaimer)

d) Attacking an opposing candidate on his or her stands on the issues is always fair game.

> **Bob Firewood Doesn't Deserve To Be Re-Elected To The State Senate:**
>
> - Firewood voted twice against funding the Highway 3 and 57 interchange
>
> - Firewood voted for the biggest tax increase in history
>
> - Firewood missed 30% of the votes in the Senate Human Services Committee
>
>
>
> **Had Enough?**
>
> Vote to Elect
>
> # PERCY PHONEBOOTH
>
> Your State Senator
>
> "Let's Put People First"
>
> (Disclaimer)

e) The Image ads are designed to convey to voters that the candidate is a likable, trustworthy person. Such ads usually have lots of photos and little copy.

YOU CAN COUNT ON JIM PINHEAD TO BE ON YOUR SIDE....

Mayor Pinhead listens to the people.

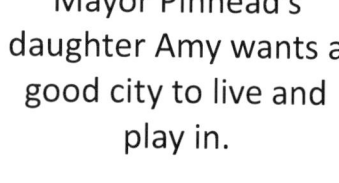

Mayor Pinhead's daughter Amy wants a good city to live and play in.

Jim Pinhead provides strong leadership.

Re-Elect MAYOR
PINHEAD

"Keeping Knittingville Moving Forward"
(disclaimer)

f) Humorous ads are generally a variation of image or issue ads.

Why are you voting for Suzie Salad for County Clerk?

| Because Sue Salad is hard working. | Sue Salad is an honest person I can trust. | I like Suzie Salad's dedication. | Well, because I AM Suzie Salad! |

Re-Elect

County Clerk
SUZIE SALAD

"Honest. Hard-Working. Dedicated"

(disclaimer)

Chapter 8: Electronic Media Advertising

The use of the electronic media for small campaign might be a bargain in more rural areas but prohibitively expensive in urban areas. As was discussed in Chapter 6, the use of the electronic media will largely depend upon the cost per voter reached.

Don't Shortchange the Print Media

Dollar for dollar, the print media will usually be more effective than the electronic media in reaching a candidate's voters in a small campaign. I say *usually*. That is simply because print media advertising can often be localized for a target audience whereas the electronic media often carries an ad well beyond where a candidate's target voters live. That is particularly true in urban areas. Placing expensive ads through the electronic media that largely reach people who cannot vote for a candidate doesn't make much sense. In some urban city-wide or county-wide races there may be some local radio stations that have a more localized broadcast "reach" and should be part of the advertising mix. If a campaign is in a more rural area there might be radio stations that broadcast 100% to voters in a candidate's election district.

When allocating scarce resources, I always advise candidates to prioritize their advertising budgets as follows:

1. The number one priority in a small campaign is <u>usually</u> the print media. A candidate must make sure to "budget backwards" and have enough money to do an adequate job in local newspapers and shoppers at the end of the campaign.

2. Radio can be a good buy if a) a candidate's ads are mainly being listened to by voters in the election district and, b) the cost per voter reached compares favorably with other media outlets.

3. Television is generally not in the mix for a small campaign because of the cost and because a political ad on TV generally is broadcast to a much broader territory than the election district a campaign is trying to penetrate.

> *For a small campaign, the usual priority is to allocate advertising funds for the print media first and radio second. In most cases TV advertising isn't in the mix.*

Save Your Ammunition

As with the print media, a campaign needs to start with a few small ads four weeks before and election and build up the total number of ads the closer you get to an election. In many cases, the availability of funds might limit a small campaign to advertising in the electronic media only during the last two weeks. That's OK. Remember that most people don't think about who they are going to vote for until the last ten days before an election.

There is one truth about electronic media advertising: a campaign has to saturate ads in order for people to register with the ad message. People mentally turn off ads on radio and TV unless they are especially well done. Unfortunately, most small campaigns cannot afford the production costs associated with the kinds of ads played during the Super Bowl each year. The only way to penetrate that mental barrier is to run electronic media ads frequently.

Some electronic media allow ads on Election Day while others do not. If a campaign can run ads on Election Day, I wouldn't recommend running ads beyond 5 PM. By then many people will have already voted so a campaign doesn't need to convince them anymore. If a campaign can run ads on Election Day, the Advertising Chairman might want to have a special one made up just for that day. Such an ad might simply be the voice of the candidate thanking the voters for their encouragement throughout the campaign and urging them to get out and vote:

> "Hi, this is Mary Clockwork, your candidate for County Clerk. I just want to thank everyone who has supported my campaign these past several months. It was wonderful meeting the people of the county during the campaign. I was especially encouraged by how many people felt that ethics in the Clerk's Office is important.
>
> Today is Election Day. Whether you support me, Mary Clockwork, for County Clerk or not, please get out and vote." (Disclaimer)

> **Hit the airwaves with the most electronic media ads right before Election Day.**

Shorter is Better

Many electronic media outlets will try pushing candidates into buying longer ads or even a half hour program. Candidates shouldn't be tempted! A candidate's election might be the most important thing in his or her life, but voters don't want to get bored listening to a long political ad. That is particularly true if a candidate's election is held during a fall General Election when the candidates for President, statewide offices and Congress are on the ballot.

In electronic media advertising it's not the length of ads that determine effectiveness, but the frequency in which ads are run and how well they are produced. I advise candidates never to buy electronic media ads greater than 30 seconds in length, including the disclaimer. If a campaign can make up a snazzy 15 second ad that stations will accept, a campaign should give that some consideration.

> *A campaign should never purchase electronic media ads that run longer than 30 second spots.*

Pay Attention to Placement

Placement of a candidate's ads is more important in the electronic media than the print media. Generally, the best time to run radio ads is during morning and afternoon drive times when people are going to and from work. The best time to run TV ads is during the evening hours from 5PM until 9PM. There are some exceptions, however. A local radio station, for example, might have a popular call-in program in the middle of the afternoon with a particularly talented host. About the only way for a campaign to determine the best times to air ads is to ask electronic media salespersons to give the Advertising Coordinator the ratings for programs throughout the day.

Having given that good advice let me say that there is an exception…some electronic media outlets will offer to run ads so cheaply during non-peak times that they can give a campaign a deal that is hard to pass up. Remember, however, to determine the "reach" and the cost per voter as was discussed in Chapter 6.

> *The placement of ads in the electronic media is more important than ad placement in the print media.*

Legal Requirements

Electronic media outlets are licensed by the Federal Government. There are two basic requirements in political advertising that a campaign needs to keep in mind:

a) Licensed electronic media must provide political candidates the lowest rates available to all advertisers through that outlet and

b) The voice of the candidate must be heard in the ad. The candidate can either speak during the body of the ad or during the disclaimer.

> *Political candidates get a cost break when advertising in the electronic media.*

The Voice, Always the Voice

Observers in the 1860's wrote that Abraham Lincoln had a high, squeaky voice. If he had run for election during our current electronic age he probably would not have been elected.

Many candidates *think* they have a good speaking voice but are often biased by a life-long appreciation of hearing their own voice; we have each been surprised by the sound of our recorded voice at some time. I have three recommendations for campaigns selecting a person to do electronic media ads: a) do NOT hire a local radio or TV personality; their voice or appearance is already familiar and people know they are doing the ad for profit, not out of political commitment, b) select someone of the opposite gender than the candidate (humanity is divided roughly 50-50 between the genders and a campaign should include both) and c) a candidate and the campaign committee must agree that the person selected has a pleasant speaking voice (and appearance for TV ads) since that individual will be the "face" of the campaign.

Most radio stations will allow a candidate and their campaign ad announcer to do ads at the studio for free or a nominal fee. They also realize that in a big district a campaign may copy the ads to send to other stations. Things are quite different when producing television ads. With television ads a campaign usually is going to have to pay production costs to an advertising agency or a TV station to have ads produced.

> *The voice in electronic media ads becomes the "face" of a campaign.*

Again, Remember K.I.S.S

While it's important to limit the number of issues discussed in a print media advertisement, it's even more important to limit the topics discussed in an electronic media advertisement.

With only 30 seconds to get a message across, there is not much time to go in-depth on issues. As was the recommendation for print media advertising, the priority in electronic media advertising is get across the candidate's name and the office he or she is running for. An actual discussion of the issues is limited.

Let me give two examples of what I mean. "Ad A" is a radio ad that covers too many issues. "Ad B" is more limited in discussing issues and concentrates more on getting the name and office of the candidate across to voters.

Ad A:

> "John Earphone stands for more accountability in the office of County Treasurer. He supports ethics reform, cross-referencing of treasury files with the state's, implementation of the 2020 management improvement program, better cooperation with the County Board's Finance Committee, weekly open door discussion coffees with taxpayers, electronic storage of records, full disclosure of county budget expenditures and more interaction with the statewide Treasury Improvement Association.
>
> Re-elect John Earphone your County Treasurer."
>
> (Disclaimer)

Ad B:

> "John Earphone is a public official who has earned your trust. From promoting ethics in government to reforming the way the County Treasurer's Office is run, County Treasurer John Earphone has proven to be a leader the voters of this county can be proud of.
>
> Your vote on November 2nd for John Earphone for County Treasurer will allow him to continue to improve the accountability and efficiency of county government.
>
> Keep a reformer in office. Re-elect John Earphone your County Treasurer.
>
> (Disclaimer)

"Ad A" has just too many references to issues. By the time a voter gets to hear the end of the ad he or she can't remember what was stated at the beginning of the ad. "Ad B" alludes to issues in a general way and emphasizes the candidate's name, the office he is seeking and gives a positive spin on the character of the candidate.

> *A campaign should avoid addressing too many issues in a short electronic media ad.*

How Many Different Ads Are Needed?

A campaign needs to run electronic media ads frequently, but it shouldn't bore listeners to tears with the same ad time after time. A campaign should produce three to four different radio ads (even less for TV). In any given day a campaign should run one ad several consecutive times and then switch its buy to another ad and run that one several consecutive times.

Let's name a campaign's ads A, B, C, and D. An advertising schedule two weeks out from the election might look like this:

Day Before Election	14	13	12	11	10	9	8
Ads to Run Each Day	A,B	A,B	C,D	C,D	A,B	A,B	C,D
Number of Each Ad, Each Day	4	4	5	5	5	6	6

Day Before Election	7	6	5	4	3	2	1
Ads to Run Each Day	C,D	A,B	C,D	A,B	C,D	A,B	C,D
Number of Each Ad, Each Day	8	8	9	9	10	10	10

> *A campaign shouldn't use too many or too few electronic media ads. Three or four different ads are about right.*

Be Prepared to Make Different Ads Quickly

Circumstances can change rapidly in an election, particularly when a campaign gets down to the final days. The opponent might attack a candidate personally or say something to deceive voters on where he or she stands on an issue. An issue might come up that could garner additional support if a candidate's position on it is known.

Thankfully, producing a radio ad is simple and can be done quickly. All you need is a person with a good speaking voice, the candidate, a script and some recording equipment.

Some media outlets have a policy of not allowing candidates to bring up new charges or issues in ads right before an election. The Advertising Coordinator should be sure to know if such a policy exists for each electronic media outlet. The election could be lost for the candidate who is unable to respond to a charge by his or her opponent through a timely ad right before the election.

> *Campaigns should be prepared to respond quickly with new ads if a new charge or issue comes up right before Election Day.*

Examples of Types of Ads for Electronic Media

As with print media advertising there are basically six different types of ads for the electronic media-Image, Issue, Endorsement, Comparison, Attack and Humorous. Below are some examples of each type of ad.

a) The Image Ad

> *"Mary Beercan is running for Mayor because she believes more can be done to make city government more efficient and accountable.*
>
> *Mary Beercan has a proven record of fighting for the taxpayers as a member of the City Council. Mary Beercan was a member of the Finance Committee that held spending to less than the rate of inflation.*
>
> *The People' Daily Horn called Mary Beercan an honest and dedicated public servant.*
>
> *On Election Day elect an honest and dedicated friend of the taxpayer. Elect Mary Beercan as your next Mayor."*
>
> (Disclaimer)

b) The Issue Ad

> *"Joe Sludgehammer is needed at the Statehouse as our State Representative. He supports comprehensive welfare reform, lower taxes and business incentives for the creation of job opportunities.*
>
> *A lot of candidates will tell you that they understand the concerns of taxpayers. Joe Sludgehammer has a record of cutting spending and taxes as a member of the County Board.*

When it comes to experience that will make the difference, there is no doubt that Joe Sludgehammer is the person we need as State Representative.

Join your friends and neighbors in voting Sludgehammer for State Representative."

(Disclaimer)

c) The Endorsement Ad

"Hi, this is Mayor Mike Foghorn. For the past eight years it has been my privilege to serve as your Mayor. We have held the line on spending and saw a growth of jobs in the community.

I want to see that progress continued. That's why I am voting for Amy Teacup as our next Mayor. Amy Teacup understands how city government works and fights for efficient government and spending restraint.

Because her fellow Councilors trust her, Amy Teacup was elected President of the Council. All ten other City Councilors have endorsed Amy Teacup for Mayor over her opponent, Mandy Moonshine.

Please join me in voting for Amy Teacup for Mayor."

(Disclaimer)

d) The Comparison Ad

"When voting for your next City Clerk considers the differences in the candidates.

George Birdhouse has experience in city government as a member of the City Council. His *opponent has none.*

George Birdhouse supported revitalization of the downtown. His opponent opposed it.

George Birdhouse voted to decrease the last budget. His opponent said he would have voted to increase it.

George Birdhouse opposed the re-routing of High 44. His opponent supported it.

George Birdhouse is simply the best candidate to be our next City Clerk. Vote for George Birdhouse for City Clerk." (Disclaimer)

e) The Attack Ad

"For Mayor, Dave Rosebud is the better candidate than Frank Bookcase.

When asked in a public forum where he would cut city spending, Frank Bookcase said he didn't know.

Frank Bookcase opposed the creation of the economic development tax district that has already brought 200 jobs to the community.

Frank Bookcase opposed downtown revitalization.

Frank Bookcase received two warnings for his questionable campaign practices from the State Elections Commission.

Don't stop progress in our community. Elect Dave Rosebud our Mayor."

(Disclaimer)

f) The Humorous Ad

(Laughter)

"Howdy partner. I live in Pinecone County, but I sure hope you folks in Maple County vote for Frank Footloose for County Commissioner. He's what we call a 'good old boy'.

Frank Footloose wants to extend water and sewer service from Maple County to Pinecone County at no expense to me and my neighbors (laughter). Now isn't that nice (more laughter).

Be sure y'all elect Frank Footloose County Commissioner instead of Sherry Seaweed. Sherry Seaweed would put the interests of Maple County first and we folks in Pinecone County wouldn't want that. That would be right neighborly of y'all (laughter)."

(Disclaimer)

> *Electronic media ads need to be short and to the point. The type of ads used depends on if the purpose of the ads are to make voters inspired, angry, thinking or laughing.*

TV and Cable TV

As you can probably surmise, I am not a big fan of the use of TV for smaller campaigns. TV is very expensive and often reaches people who can't vote for a local candidate anyway. If a smaller, localized campaign is in a general election with a lot of higher offices on the ballot its ads will get lost in all the political advertising "clutter". If a campaign committee has tons of money for boosting its candidate and wants to use TV, I would suggest that it produce only one or two 30 second spots and run them as frequently as it can afford. Such ads should be "image" or "comparison" ads that don't go in-depth on issues but rather convey the impression of what a fine, honest, likable, hardworking person they will find in the candidate.

In some jurisdictions there is a local cable TV station. The viewing audience for such stations is usually small. It may be, however, that the costs for advertising on such an outlet is so inexpensive that throwing a few dollars at the station may make sense.

> *Using TV advertising is great if a campaign has lots of money. For many smaller campaigns it is not a good investment.*

Digital Advertising and Information Technology

Even a small campaign is wise to explore the vast opportunities of communicating with voters through digital technology. Whether the sophisticated technology that is available today is used for a web page, email targeting, advertising on social media platforms or periodic issue postings, it is important for a campaign to have a person on board who is adept with digital technology.

In considering a digital technology component of a campaign, it's important to keep in mind some basic principles of advertising through digital platforms:

a) Digital marketing, like other advertising vehicles, needs to convey a positive image of the candidate and address issues that resonate with voters.
b) Digital platforms should allow for two-way communications between the campaign and voters.
c) An important purpose in the use of digital technology is to create networks between voters and between voters and the campaign.
d) Because of the pervasive use of electronic devices often create "information overload", it's important that political ads and messaging be short, informative and attention-grabbing.
e) Digital technology is most effective if it is used to target specific voters or groups of voters.

A campaign can either disseminate its political messaging to the general population in a specific area (election district) or it can apply a more refined approach to reach specific voters based on data collection outlined in demographic, economic, behavioral or psychological profiling. There are many businesses that collect data that they then sell to marketers and advertisers. Individuals are then targeted because of their age, gender, political affiliations or leanings, buying habits, income levels, religious beliefs and hundreds of other indicators. For a very small campaign, hiring a data collection business to help the campaign target voters might be out of the question, but should be investigated. If you are running for a partisan office, your party may already have lists of the voters you need to target.

If political advertising in the print media, handouts, and traditional electronic media needs to be concise and short on copy and long on image, the principles of K.I.S.S. discussed in Chapter 5 are even more important to keep in mind when employing digital technology in a campaign. Most people will look at a political ad on social media platforms for only for a few seconds. That requires that any messaging be short and simple.

Chapter 6 talked about the various types of ads that a campaign can employ in generating support for its candidate. All the ad types discussed earlier can be used in social media platforms, but they must be even more concise than they would be if they are used in a newspaper or in a 30 second radio ad. Here are some examples:

a) Image Ad:
- Candidate A supports our seniors. (Picture of candidate with seniors)

b) Endorsement Ad:
- Senator Rockhead endorses Candidate A. (Photo of the senator and the candidate)

c) Issue Ad:
- Candidate A supports more money for city streets. (Photo of potholes)

d) Comparison Ad:
- Candidate A supports repairs to the park dam. Candidate B voted against repairs (Photo of dam)

e) Attack Ad:
- Candidate B voted AGAINST lowering property taxes. (Bad photo of Candidate B)

f) Humorous Ad:
- Seriously? Candidate B is for better civility at City Hall? Only when everyone agrees with him. (Photo of two people laughing)

A good way to find out what issues resonate with voters would be to use digital technology to conduct an issue survey. A Facebook® or web page survey, for example, might contain ten short issues (education, environment, roads, taxes, etc.) and ask readers to rank the importance of those issues.

Posting videos on a campaign's web page or social media page like YouTube® or Facebook® can be a real asset in introducing a candidate or in having the candidate discusses the issues of a campaign. Like the general rule for TV and radio ads, posting videos should not run over 30 seconds. With the technology in modern "smart phones", a quality video can be produced and posted with a campaign volunteer's phone.

An effective tool with the use of a web page or other social media is the ability for two-way communication. Many visitors to a candidate's digital platforms might have questions about the candidate's position on issues, suggestions on how the campaign can be more effective, want information on how they can help and simply desire to speak out on some issue or problem.

At the very least, a campaign should have an internet web page. Examples of political web pages and templates for designing a custom site are readily available on the internet. A candidate web page should contain a statement from the candidate, a short list of issues and priorities, news releases or reactions to issues, lots of photos of the candidate and his or her family, a bio, videos of the candidate meeting people or making statements, and places to click for donating and volunteering. Asking web page visitors for their email address allows the campaign to keep in touch with people interested in the campaign and provides a means of contacting them for support.

A candidate's web page should have frequent changes in entries including new photos and videos, candidate schedule updates, news releases or candidate statements and any new information on how people can get involved in the campaign. Campaign literature, ads and postings in other social media should continually direct people to the web page. Supporters using social media should urge their contacts to "like" or "subscribe" to the candidate's web page.

Many social media platforms like Facebook® and Google® have political advertising packages available that target specific audiences in a geographic area. Advertising through them are relatively inexpensive. Even a small campaign should investigate advertising costs and the "reach" in targeting a specific group of voters.

A good way for a campaign to have a continual conversation with voters is to create an interactive blog either as a stand-alone web entity or as a page on one of the social media platforms. As people join the blog, there will be more interactions with the candidate and discussions of specific issues. Blogs can get to be lively and controversial, so a campaign might want to encourage specific individuals to post comments that are "on message" with the candidate's issues and beliefs.

Posting daily "tweets" on Twitter® is a good way for a candidate to ask for volunteers, talk about issues, and announce schedules for campaigning and events and the like. Twitter® can be considered a "miniblog" since the discussion of issues is usually boiled down to a sentence or two.

Finally, don't forget that lists of actual voters may be available from your local election clerk or your state's election administration agency in an electronic format. Those voter lists can be acquired for a nominal fee and are usually available on a ward, district or county-wide basis. They usually contain the name and address of each voter, when a person voted in a specific election and oftentimes the phone number or email address of voters. Those lists are invaluable in campaigning door-to-door, sending out mailers and soliciting donations and volunteers. When ordering electronic voter files, order lists that are the most current and ones that best pertain to your election. If you are running in a spring election, for example, you would want to get the voter lists from the most recent spring election.

We live in an "electronic age" where the sharing of information and the influencing of voters in a campaign will increasingly occur through the use of digital technology. Thankfully, sharing information, discussing issues, creating positive images for a candidate and campaign advertising are readily available and generally affordable for smaller campaigns using digital technology.

> *Campaign use of the Internet and popular digital platforms is inexpensive or free and likely a necessity in reaching online users in most modern elections.*

Chapter 9: Campaign Materials and Mailings

Regardless of the size of a campaign, a candidate needs to get his or her name and issues before the voters. Signs, handouts and other campaign materials need to be made or purchased for that purpose. A campaign should consider direct mailings of letters and post cards. Whatever campaign materials and mailings are used, a campaign should stick with the same campaign colors, logo design and slogan throughout.

Types of Letters

There are four basic types of letters that campaigns use for direct mailings to voters:

a) The Candidate Letter: This is normally a "from the heart" letter from the candidate expressing why he or she is running for office and what the candidate hopes to accomplish if elected. Most often it will have the candidate's name and photo boldly across a banner space at the top of the letter. Such a letter should be fairly brief but get the major messages across that the candidate wants to convey.

b) The Endorsement Letter: The endorsement letter should be signed by prominent leaders of the community. Having controversial individuals sign a letter can end up hurting a campaign. If a candidate can get individuals who would normally support his or her opponent to sign an endorsement letter all the better.

c) The Informational Letter: This type may not look like a letter at all. It may look more like an ad that would be in a newspaper. In fact, it could be a replica of one of the ads the campaign is using in the print media. As was discussed in Chapter 6, there are six major types of print media ads that could be employed: Image, Endorsement, Issue, Comparison, Humorous, and Attack. Any one of these ad types can be incorporated into an informational letter. The main purpose of an informational letter is to inform voters on the issues or point out the differences between the candidates.

d) **The Targeted Letter:** The targeted letter is intended to appeal to a specific segment of the voting public. A targeted letter to physicians might discuss just medical issues. A targeted letter to businesspersons might just talk about business issues. A targeted letter to farmers might just discuss agricultural issues. If a candidate has been endorsed by some labor, business, professional or social group, the campaign should ask that group to send a targeted letter to their members, separate from the campaign's mailings.

No matter what type of letter a campaign decides to send out, keep in mind K.I.S.S. I would not recommend that any direct mail letter be over one page, printed on one side. If a campaign letter gets too wordy many voters will just simply toss it into the recycling bin or garbage without reading the first line.

Letters should be kept brief.

Post Cards and Flyers

Post cards are relatively inexpensive to print and distribute. Mailed flyers like 8.5" x 11" folded once or twice are fairly popular.

Post cards are great for last minute reminders to voters to get out and vote. A card with a candidate's name, picture, office sought, and a simple message like "Don't forget that Tuesday is Election Day. I would appreciate your support for County Sheriff" might be all you need. A candidate should consider sending a last-minute post card especially to areas of his or her greatest strength. Those are the areas that a candidate needs a good voter turnout.

Flyers can be either mailed or left at homes by volunteers going door-to-door. While observing campaigns over the years I have seen more bad flyers than good ones. So, what's the main problem? Too many words! Flyers should mention issues only briefly and contain several pictures of the candidate meeting voters or with his or her family.

> *Post cards and flyers are inexpensive and effective if they are not too "wordy."*

Mailing Tactics

If a campaign does decide to do mailings with letters, post cards or flyers, there are a few things to consider besides the content of such mailings:

a) If a campaign is going to do mass mailings, consideration should be given to getting a Bulk Mailing Permit. Having the permit number printed on the mailing might save a lot of time and money over putting a stamp on each piece being mailed. If using a Bulk Mailing Permit be sure to allow for extra time for the Post Office to process your mailing.

b) Post Office locations have pre-stamped post cards and mailing envelopes available for purchase. Using these materials saves time.

c) Avoid using mailings to raise funds for the campaign. Generally, such mailings barely bring in enough money to cover printing and mailing expenses. The exception would be if the mailing stated that funds were needed and that someone would be making a following-up contact in requesting a donation. The campaign must make sure that the follow-up contact is made just a few days after the mailing is received by potential donors.

d) "Timing is everything in politics," as the old saying goes. A campaign generally should not get mailings out until the last few weeks or days of a campaign. The exception is if a mailing is sent earlier to "introduce" the candidate to the public or to conduct an opinion survey.

e) If a campaign can get enough volunteers to help, sort any mailing by zip code before delivering the mailing to the Post Office. That will better ensure that your mailing will be delivered in a timely fashion.

f) Don't be afraid to go parochial. A candidate can use a last-minute mailing to appeal to his or her ethnic group, religion, community or home county to attract votes. During my first campaign I sent out a simple post card to voters in my home county in my eight-county legislative district. It simply stated that it was over 100 years since someone from my home county was elected to the State Senate and asked the question "Isn't It about Time?" It worked!

g) If sending a targeted mailing to a specific group of voters, make sure that it is only mailed to your targeted audience. Sending a target letter that was meant for dentists to an electrician or farmer can lose support.

h) Avoid attacking a group of voters in your district even if you don't send a mailing to members of that group. You can be sure your opponent will get a copy of your letter to the group you are attacking. It is generally not a good idea to blast anybody but your opponent!

i) If a general mailing is being sent out, make sure that it is getting to the homes of actual voters. Why waste the money sending a mailer to people who don't vote? In most jurisdictions there are poll lists of registered voters. Some of those lists are available electronically making it easier to affix addresses to letters, post cards and flyers. If you can, get poll lists for the last general election. Those are the people that a candidate needs to communicate with. In many states, voters must designate that they are an independent or indicate a party preference when they initially register to vote. A candidate running for a partisan office would be wise to do a special mailing to people registered as supporting his or her political party.

j) If running for a partisan office a campaign should ascertain if there is a list of voters supporting the candidates of the his or her political party. Oftentimes political parties or candidates running for higher office conduct phone surveys to determine which voters are supporting them. Sending a special mailing to those targeted voters can be highly productive.

> *The most efficient and productive way to do mailings is to send communications to targeted voters.*

Yard Signs

Unless a candidate's election district is in a densely populated urban setting (no yards), yard signs are indispensable for most campaigns. They are inexpensive and have a bold impact. At a minimum, a campaign should try to place at least 20 yard signs for every 500 homes. Personally, I prefer the corrugated plastic signs that can be reused. Paper signs, however, are considerably cheaper.

Some political advisors tell candidates to start getting yard signs out months ahead of the election to increase name recognition. I disagree. Yard signs that get out too early tend to blend into the background and get unnoticed once a person sees them a few times. Isn't the purpose of a campaign to have maximum name recognition on Election Day? There's another advantage for holding off...If an opponent doesn't see too many yard signs early in the campaign, he or she might be lulled into thinking that a challenging candidate isn't working hard enough. That's good.

Here's the formula I used in my successful campaigns and advised other candidates to use. Place 10% of your signs four weeks before the election, 20% three weeks before the election, 30% two weeks before the election and 40% the week before the election. Follow that formula and I guarantee that it will look like there's a strong groundswell of support for a candidate just when he or she wants to have the maximum impact (Election Day).

A Yard Sign Coordinator should concentrate on the placement of yard signs at the most strategic locations during the first few waves of sign distribution. Those locations include major thoroughfares and intersections with stop lights or stop signs.

Throughout a campaign people will volunteer to take signs on behalf of a candidate. A campaign should keep their names and addresses for later delivery of signs. When a candidate is going door to door or otherwise meeting people, he or she shouldn't be afraid to ask people to take a sign if they indicate support.

Probably the easiest way to get yard signs placed is for campaign volunteers to simply walk down a street with armloads of signs. When they see a good location, they should knock on the door of the home and ask the resident if they can place a sign. If the resident says "yes" then the volunteer should immediately place a sign.

DO NOT place signs on highway rights-of-way or in ditches next to roadways. What that tells a passing motorist is that the candidate: a) doesn't like following the law since placing signs in such locations is generally illegal, b) doesn't care about the environment by littering along a roadway and c) doesn't have too much support if people won't take his or her signs and put them on their own property.

> *Campaign yard signs are relatively inexpensive, and they are very effective.*

Large Home-made Signs

An inexpensive and effective means to get a candidate's name visible is to make signs out of 4' x 4' or 4' x 8' sheets of plywood. Such signs should be painted to look identical to a candidate's other signs with a use of stencil (including the disclaimer). Place such large signs only in the most visible locations. Because large signs can be a problem in a strong wind it is important to secure them properly. It is highly recommended that large wood signs be attached to metal or wooden posts that are anchored in the ground.

Another way to make large home-made signs is to paint large bed sheets and have them secured to the sides of barns, homes or other large structures. It might be a problem painting sheets to look exactly like a candidate's other signs, but the lettering in one of the colors of a candidate's signs will suffice. Be sure to sew a disclaimer patch at the bottom.

Home-made signs on plywood or even bed sheets can make a big impact for a candidate.

Store Placards

If a candidate has strong support in the business community his campaign might want to have store placards printed up. Such signs should be printed on poster-board, look identical to a candidate's yard signs and be 8.5" x 11" or larger.

If a campaign decides to go with store placards it would be best if a businessperson volunteers to go from business to business in distributing them. Placing such signs in store windows, in back of a counter or bar or on a bulletin board will get lots of notice. A campaign must make sure that permission is given by the store owner or manager before placing such signs.

> *If there are a lot of small businesses in an election district, a campaign might want to consider store placards.*

Billboards

If a campaign really wants to get people's attention, it should rent some billboards. A campaign should rent such billboards only for the last month before the election and stay with the same colors and design that are used on other signs and handouts. In many rural areas, production costs of the sign materials and renting the billboards through a local outdoor advertising company is relatively inexpensive.

A new trend in the billboard advertising is electronic billboards. They certainly get attention, but they may be too expensive for most smaller and medium sized campaigns.

> *Billboards get noticed and should be considered.*

Bumper Stickers

For smaller campaigns I wouldn't recommend purchasing bumper stickers. They are hard to get on cars and much of the time someone will take one and put it in a glove compartment until after the election. There is an exception to my recommendation, however... If a campaign has enough enthusiastic volunteers who will work parking lots, ask drivers if they want a sticker and then putting them on right then and there, then go for it.

If a campaign decides to use bumper stickers it should order vinyl ones not paper. Vinyl stickers hold up better than paper ones and are easier to peel off after the election.

A campaign should NEVER put a sticker on a bumper without the permission of the vehicle owner, unless a campaign volunteer wants his teeth knocked out.

> *Bumper stickers probably aren't a good investment for many smaller campaigns.*

Cartops

There are two kinds of ready-made cartops on the market that are frequently used by campaigns: a) small Styrofoam cartops that adhere to a car roof with sticky pads on the corners and b) large two or three-sided ones that are attached to a frame and secured to a car roof drain gutters (if equipped) with cables or ropes.

I have used both. In my opinion the small Styrofoam ones are worthless. Some of them are blank and require a campaign to affix bumper stickers. If a campaign hadn't intended on getting bumper stickers that can be a problem. Even if a campaign's sign is printed on the small cartops, they still are a bad investment. They often blow off cars and are lost and they are too small to be read by passing motorists.

If a campaign is going to use cartops, it should purchase the large ones that are available through many campaign supply companies. If placed on cars that are parked along major streets or in large parking lots, they have a big impact.

I have often seen candidates in small campaigns make their own homemade cartops. That's an option that may be cheaper than purchasing them through a campaign supply company. If that route is selected, a campaign must make sure that such signs look the same as its other signs and contain the disclaimer.

> *Cartops can be effective, but only use the larger types.*

Door-To-Door Handout

A candidate needs some piece of literature to give voters when he or she or volunteers are going door-to-door campaigning. Usually that is a doorknob hanger or a brochure. If a candidate is using a doorknob hanger his picture and the office he is seeking should on one side and a brief listing of his issues should on the other. If a candidate is using a brochure, I wouldn't recommend anything larger than an 8.5" x 11" sheet that is printed and folded two to three times. The candidate's picture and the office sought should be on the front flap. The rest of the flyer should be filled with lots of pictures of the candidate meeting voters and a brief listing of issues.

Which door-to-door handout to use? A brochure has the advantage of accommodating more pictures and copy. A brochure can also be used for a handout at other events like coffees, dinners and community festivals. The advantage of a door knob hanger is that it generally is cheaper to produce and can be secured to a door knob when nobody is at home (a brochure has to be stuck inside a storm or screen door, or attached to a door knob with a fastener like a rubber band).

> ***Every candidate needs a brochure or doorknob hanger for door-to-door campaigning.***

Example Brochure:
Outside Copy

Yes! I want to help elect Frank. I Will:

- ☐ Contribute
- ☐ Hold a Coffee
- ☐ Write Letters
- ☐ Take a Yard Sign
- ☐ Go Door-To-Door

Name:_____

Address:_____

Phone:_____

Send To:
Citizens For Honesty
1033 Main Street
Crabappletree, PA

(Authorized and Paid for by Citizens for Honesty Committee, Pat Granite, Treasurer.)

Elect

FRANK FIELDSTONE

Your Mayor

"A Mayor You Can Trust!"

Inside Copy

- Frank Fieldstone is a family man who cares about the future of Crabappletree.

- Frank Fieldstone has experience with five terms of the City Council.

- Frank Fieldstone led the way to reduce taxes.

- Frank Fieldstone fought against the costly landfill project.

- Frank Fieldstone will be "a Mayor you can trust."

You can trust Frank Fieldstone to fight for:

- Lower Taxes

- Job Development

- Downtown Revitalization

- Clean Local Government

- Better Public Safety

Elect

FIELDSTONE
Mayor

Example Doorknob Hangar Front:

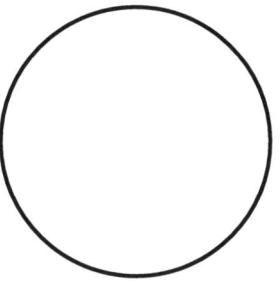

MARY SMALLMOUTH

County Treasurer

"Your Money is Safe with a Smallmouth"

Example Doorknob Hangar Back:

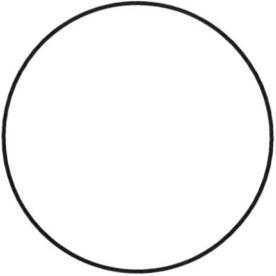

As County Treasurer, Mary Smallmouth will:

- Fight for a full recovery of unspent funds
- Open finance records to the public
- Modernize the county budget process
- Demand that delinquent taxpayers pay up
- Support a new audit of county funds

MARY SMALLMOUTH

County Treasurer

*(Authorized and Paid for by Smallmouth Good Government Committee,
H. Bottomlip, Chairman)*

Small Identification Handout

If a candidate plans to campaign at entrances to workplaces, in front of stores and at community festivals and picnics, he or she needs a small handout the size of a normal business card. The candidate's picture and the office sought should be on one side. The other side should be used for something that will cause a voter to keep the card. A calendar is a popular option as is a schedule of a hometown sports team.

> *A candidate needs a small handout that a voter will keep.*

Other Handouts

Many campaign supply companies can manufacture other handouts that a campaign might want to consider like matches, fingernail files, key chains and pencils. If these types of items are used a campaign must make sure to check if they are legal. Some states and local jurisdictions have prohibitions on candidates passing out "things of value."

> *A campaign must make sure that campaign handouts are legal.*

Chapter 10: Events and Appearances

Unless a candidate is running unopposed, he or she usually cannot win an election unless there is a personal interaction with voters. Voters want to know a candidate and what he or she stands for. When voters get in the voting booth, they have to feel better about voting for a candidate than his or her opponent.

Door-To-Door

If a candidate is running for Governor or the Congress, he or she can't possibly go door-to-door to reach thousands or millions of voters. If, however, a candidate is running for a local office or a state legislative seat, door-to-door canvassing is ESSENTIAL. There is nothing more important than meeting the people. Voters might not agree with a candidate on every issue, but if they met the candidate, they are more likely to vote for him or her on Election Day. In my first race for the State Senate in Wisconsin I spent six months knocking on 30,000 doors and lost 70 pounds. It was grueling, but effective.

Consider these basics in the important function of doing door-to-door campaigning:

a) A candidate must always have a handout like a brochure or doorknob hanger to leave at each residence as was discussed in Chapter 9.

b) A candidate should NOT campaign door-to-door before 9 AM or after sundown. Campaigning too early may roust people from bed. Campaigning too late may disturb people from relaxing after a long day at work and can potentially be dangerous.

c) The candidate and his supporters going door-to-door should always use a *medium* knock on the door. Never knock hard or ring the doorbell! If people are in an adjacent area of the house, they usually will hear a *medium* knock and will respond. If they are sleeping, in bed sick, disabled or at the other end of the house and are summoned with a loud knock or the doorbell they will probably be irritated. An unhappy voter is a voter who just got pushed over to the candidate's opponent.

d) It's a good idea for a candidate to carry MACE or other appropriate repellant in case of a dog attack. I found that small dogs were more likely to bite at my ankles or try to attack than larger dogs. That's just my experience, however. I sure would not like to be attacked by a larger dog. Never try to pet a dog. Above all, never go into a yard where you see a dog sleeping even if it is on a chain ("Let sleeping dogs lay" is an old expression that campaigners better heed).

e) Candidates should keep greetings short when going door-to-door. Something simple like this works just fine:

"Good afternoon. I am Pete Pothole and I am running for County Treasurer. I just wanted to stop by to introduce myself and to leave you this information (hand voter brochure or doorknob hanger). Do you have any questions of me? (Only one in 20 people will have a question). Thanks for your time. I hope I can count on your support."

It cannot be emphasized enough how important it

is for a candidate to keep a presentation short. Most people do not want to get into a long discussion about politics on their front porch. It's "Mission Accomplished" if a candidate is able to hand a voter some information and give that person an opportunity to ask questions. Most voters will be flattered that a candidate even stopped by their home to ask for their vote. Remember K.I.S.S.

f) A candidate's slipping in a compliment about how cute a voter's little kid is or how he likes the voter's flower bed is perfectly appropriate. The candidate just shouldn't dwell on the compliment, however. The purpose in stopping by the home of a voter is to get their vote, not to get into a discussion of genetics or landscape architecture.

g) No matter what the geographical size an election district, it's a good idea for a candidate to work door-to-door on one area for a few days and then move to another area. It may be that the candidate will need to come back to finish off visiting some community or neighborhood later on. The important thing is to create a "buzz" that the candidate is working hard and campaigning everywhere. It will drive his or her opponent nuts.

h) Campaigning door-to-door can be hard physically. If an election district is small, getting to every house shouldn't be a problem for most candidates. If a candidate is running for office in a large election district, however, hitting every door personally can be a challenge. That's where a campaign's local Volunteer Coordinator comes in. If the campaign can recruit volunteers to walk door-to-door with the candidate, his or her job is reduced substantially. The candidate can take one side of the street and a volunteer the other. If the volunteer runs into a voter with a question for the candidate, the candidate can run across the street to meet the voter. If not, the team can move on. A candidate's spouse or children make great partners in going door-to-door also.

i) A candidate should start door-to-door campaigning early in the campaign in areas <u>of his or her greatest strength</u>. A campaign needs to build early identification and support in areas that are most likely to vote for its candidate. Those are the areas that most likely will supply a campaign with the most volunteers and campaign contributions. A candidate should finish the door-to-door campaign in areas of <u>his or her greatest weakness</u>. A candidate needs the voters in those areas to have a fresh memory that he or she visited them as they go into the voting booth.

j) A candidate needs to prioritize door-to-door time. A candidate likely will do well in areas of his strength even if he doesn't hit every door. He cannot shortchange spending time hitting every door in areas of his weakness, however. A candidate has to remember that for every vote he switches from his opponent to himself, mathematically he gains 2 votes, not 1. Apartment buildings and mobile home parks should be campaigned in only if the candidate has the time. The voter turnout is usually much lower in such residential settings than in areas of single-family housing units. If an election district has pockets of large concentrations of senior citizens, those areas should be hit hard. Those seniors vote!

k) People campaigning door-to-door should dress appropriately. Wearing a suit or a flowing dress and fancy shoes will look strange or even ridiculous. Campaigners should wear casual clothing and comfortable walking shoes.

l) There has never been a political campaign in the history of the United States where a candidate has not run into a verbal assault from some individual. Sometimes such encounters can be downright rude. A candidate should try to be as gracious as he can. He should avoid getting into an argument. He should try to extricate himself as soon as possible. A lot of times people trying to pick a fight with a candidate don't vote, dislike all politicians and/or support the opponent. A candidate should ignore such individuals and not let unpleasant experiences get him down. A candidate should bounce back quickly. When he knocks on the next door the resident might offer to take a yard sign or hold a coffee.

> *Going door-to-door is the most important investment in time that a candidate can make. It is essential in small campaigns.*

Coffees

There are two groups of people that a candidate wants to reach through coffee receptions at private residences: a) the "movers and shakers" and b) people living in areas where going door-to-door is impracticable. Some general rules of coffees:

a) When I campaigned in an eight-county legislative district I had a Coffee Coordinator in each county. The important thing is to have a Coffee Coordinator who can recruit respected people in each community or neighborhood to hold a coffee.

b) Coffees should be rather informal. Coffee hosts should be instructed by the Coffee Coordinator to just be able to: a) invite 20-30 of their friends, neighbors, professional colleagues or co-workers to the event (preferably by verbal confirmation of attendance), b) have coffee and cookies for refreshments and c) be willing to open their homes for only about an hour.

c) A candidate should stay at a coffee only about an hour. After arriving, the candidate should greet the host and each guest, talk for about 10 minutes and then open things up for questions. After 45 minutes a candidate should make some brief closing remarks, ask for the support of attendees and then depart. It makes it easier to leave if a volunteer or spouse discreetly tells that candidate that it's time to leave for the next appointment.

d) A campaign should send out a news release to local media if there are to be a series of coffees in a particular community or county on a particular day. The Coffee Coordinator(s) should make sure that hosts are cognizant of that. Hosts shouldn't worry. In all the hundreds of coffees conducted on my behalf in six campaigns I can count on one hand the number of people who just walked in off the street to attend a coffee at a private home. Sending out a release about a campaign's coffee receptions is just a means of getting free publicity and making people feel like the candidate is approachable.

e) A candidate should leave campaign materials such as a brochure or handout at each coffee event. It is also essential to leave a card that attendees can use to sign up to volunteer to take a yard sign, distribute literature or donate to the campaign.

f) A candidate should use coffees to make statements that are the basis of news releases to be sent throughout his or her election district. Coffees are legitimate "campaign events" just as much as a speech before the local Rotary Club or union meeting. Heck, a Coffee Coordinator could invite in the local media with the permission of the candidate and the coffee host. Who knows, a local reporter may cover the event and take a photo that will appear in the next edition.

g) A candidate must appreciate the fact that hosts have to put in quite a bit of work to have friends and/or community leaders visit their homes. They have to clean the house, send out invitations, get refreshments ready and serve as hosts for their guests and a current or future government leader. A candidate should praise his or her coffee hosts and leave a little gift upon departing. I used to give out fancy handkerchiefs to my lady coffee hosts. A thank you letter or call after the event would also be wise. Coffee hosts that are respected in the community and appreciated by the candidate will speak well of the candidate long after the event.

> *Organizing coffees at the homes of respected community leaders is a great way for a candidate to meet voters, especially ones that are otherwise hard to reach.*

"Town Hall" Receptions

"Town Hall" or "Listening Session" events are very similar to "coffees" with the big differences being that they are held at public places rather than residential homes and invitations are either mailed or delivered by volunteers door-to-door to people living in a targeted neighborhood rather then sent to specific individuals. Other than that, the format is the same with the candidate greeting attendees, coffee and cookies being available, the candidate making opening and closing remarks and time set aside for questions and answers. Like "coffees", they should be designed to last about an hour.

Parades

Holiday and community festival parades are a wonderful way for a candidate to be seen by hundreds or thousands of voters. I used to dread the coming of Independence Day because I knew that my wife, kids and I would have to rush to three to four July 4th parades and that we would be too tired to go to evening fireworks when we got back home.

A campaign should follow these suggestions for a successful appearance in parades by a candidate:

a) People want to see the candidate and his or her family. They can't do that if the candidate is sitting in the back of a car that is dimly lit. A campaign should judge the audience...If the parade is in an affluent neighborhood a nice convertible will work. If the parade is in a less affluent community have a volunteer get an older convertible or pickup truck. Riding on the back of a hay wagon pulled by a tractor is just fine in a small, rural community.

b) The vehicle entry should be decorated with patriotic materials. American flags taped to the front fenders are good. Bunting on the front and back hoods work well.

c) Include in the vehicle the candidate's spouse, children and/or supporters. People riding in the entry should dress informally, but not sloppily. A dress for ladies and a tie for men are always appropriate. Red, white and blue always work even if it's not the 4th of July. People associate red, white and blue with patriotism and elections.

d) If a candidate feels comfortable with it, he or she might want to take one side of the street and have the spouse, children, or volunteers take the other side of the street and shake hands and pass out literature the entire parade route while keeping pace with the campaign's entry in a parade. If a candidate doesn't feel comfortable doing that then at least he or she should wave and smile at parade-goers.

e) A candidate should expect to run into hecklers or people who want to argue in almost any parade route. Some of them are supporters of the opposition. Some of them just hate people in politics or people running for public office. Some of them are just plain jerks. A candidate should ignore them and look the other way as if his or her hearing aid batteries are low, and the catcall was not audible. It does a candidate's campaign and blood pressure no good to get in a discussion with such individuals.

f) In a race for a partisan office, many people may vote for a candidate while not supporting the other candidates of his or her party. Unless a candidate is running for office in an area dominated by his or her political party, it probably is best that a candidate present himself separately from other candidates of his or her party.

g) If a candidate is in an open vehicle it's important to have a respected individual in the driver's seat. People will look at the candidate and his family, but they will also look at the person supporting the candidate behind the wheel.

h) A campaign must make sure to have signs on either side of a parade entry that spells out the candidate's name and the office that he or she is holding or running for. If the candidate is going to do many parades during the campaign season it would be wise to purchase magnetic signs that can just be slapped on either side of vehicle before each parade.

> *A candidate should get to as many community parades in an election district as possible. It's a great way for hundreds or thousands of voters to see a candidate.*

County Fairs and Festivals

Working the entrances to the grounds of fairs and festivals is a great place to meet people. Generally, all a candidate or his supporters need to do is to hand out a small card or flyer, shake hands and ask people for their vote. Most people going through the entrance gate of a county fair or community festival really don't want to spend much time talking with a candidate. That's good. The purpose isn't to educate the voters. The purpose is to merely meet voters and give them some handout.

Campaigning at the entrances to fairs and festivals is preferable to walking around the grounds. At entrances, a candidate is meeting people only once. If a candidate walks around the grounds of a community event, chances are the candidate will forget who he or she met two hours before and will be greeting some people again. These people will not be pleased that the candidate thought so little of them that he or she didn't remember meeting them previously. Worse yet, the candidate may look foolish in reacting to the embarrassing situation.

A booth at a community event is ok but is not as effective as having the candidate meet voters at an event entrance.

At an event entrance, a candidate can interact with almost all attendees. In a booth, a candidate can only interact with those people who choose to walk up and meet the candidate.

People littering a community event grounds with a candidate's handout can be a problem. That's why I always preferred using a small card rather than brochure at such events. Most people will keep a small card with a calendar or sports schedule on it while that is not the case with a political brochure.

> **The best way for a candidate to meet people at a community event is to stand at the entrance.**

Picnics

Church, social, and neighborhood events are productive in meeting voters. A candidate should just go around each table, shake hands and distribute a handout. If the candidate happens to belong to the same religious denomination or group, then he or she should say so. It will be all the better for the candidate if a campaign can persuade a respected group leader or elder to go around and introduce the candidate to the group members.

A candidate shouldn't be afraid to attend gatherings of groups that normally wouldn't support him, usually because of party affiliation. Participants will appreciate the fact that a candidate decided to come to meet them and hear their concerns.

> *Picnics are a great way for a candidate to meet many voters in a relaxed setting.*

Phoning Voters

Larger campaigns for Governor or U.S. Senate often rely on party volunteers to call voters who support their candidate, especially in the few days before Election Day. Those calls often are follow-ups to earlier surveys to determine which candidate or party a voter is leaning toward supporting. Many elections come down to not which candidate or platform citizens gravitate to, but which voters show up at the polls. Many larger campaigns hire companies that direct recorded messages to targeted voters, called "robo-calls."

I have never been a real fan of phone campaigning, especially with recorded messages. Getting those calls is irritating. They must work, however, since large campaigns continue to use them.

For smaller campaigns for local, county or legislative offices, setting up phone banks with volunteers or hiring out firms to disseminate recorded messages can be too expensive or impractical. If a candidate is running for a more localized partisan office, he or she might just rely on the party to do a general "get out the vote" phoning effort to its members.

If a candidate is running in a smaller campaign, I have this suggestion: the candidate should personally call 10 voters a night, preferably to people who are on poll lists and who actually vote. If a candidate makes 10 calls a day that is over 300 voters called per month. In the six months before the election that is 1,800 voters who are contacted. If a candidate's constituency contains 5,000 real voters that can have a huge impact. Besides, those people who are contacted will mention it to 2-3 of their friends and neighbors.

> *For a smaller campaign, personal phone calls from a candidate can have a huge impact.*

Workplace and Store Entrances

I once woke up at 4 AM and traveled 60 miles to be in time for the 7 AM shift change at a plant gate that had a lot of voters. Greeting workers at plant gates (inbound and outbound) is a staple in many election districts. Workers appreciate the extra effort a candidate makes to meet them.

I found that passing out a small card with the candidate's picture and office sought on one side and a calendar or local sports schedule on the other worked best in such situations. When going on private property of a business it is always appropriate to ask the business owner or manager for permission to campaign on the property.

Similar to the plant gate is the store or mall entrance. The procedure for the candidate is the same: a) say "hi", b) state your name and the office you are running for, c) hand out a brochure or small card and d) ask for their vote.

When campaigning at a factory gate or retail entrance it's a good idea for a candidate to have a volunteer or two to help out. Sometimes the number of people entering or leaving the entrance can be so great that a candidate working alone will miss a lot of voters.

> *The best way to campaign at the entrances to workplaces or stores is to have a small card to pass out.*

Organizational Meetings

The Scheduling Coordinator should book a candidate into as many meetings of business, labor, civic and fraternal organizations as possible. Attending organizational meetings is a way to meet many voters at once. Sometimes they also provide a candidate an opportunity to speak and get a news release out.

Ideally, a candidate should arrive early and greet organizational members as they are entering the meeting place. It would be good for a candidate to give each member a handout as he or she greets them.

The Scheduling Coordinator should find out if a candidate can address the group that he or she will be visiting. If allowed, the candidate should be prepared to talk for no more than 15 minutes and then open it up to questions. If the campaign is sending out a news release based on a candidate's comments before a group, the candidate must make sure that he or she covers all the issues and quotes that will be in the release as was covered in Chapter 4.

Many organizations don't allow political candidates to give speeches during election campaigns. That shouldn't stop a candidate! Local supporters should find a member of such organizations who will take the candidate to a meeting and introduce the candidate as a guest.

Finally, a candidate shouldn't be afraid to attend meetings of groups that might normally be hostile to his or her candidacy. Remember that if a candidate can convert one voter of the opponent, he or she gains two votes mathematically. The important thing in attending such meetings is for the candidate to "keep cool". Many people in such audiences will respect the fact that a candidate was at least willing to meet with them. They might not vote for the candidate, but they might not oppose his or her candidacy as strongly either.

> *A candidate should attend as many organizational meetings as possible and try to speak at them if that is permitted.*

Debates

Candidate debates or forums are a staple of modern politics no matter what the size of a campaign. A person running for public office should expect that. A few suggestions:

- Fairly early in a campaign a candidate should get out in front by challenging his or her opponent to debate the issues. The candidate should send out a news release based on a written request made to the League of Women Voters or other civic group to sponsor such gatherings. In many cases local groups will normally set up candidate forums anyway. Why not beat them to it by sending out a news release and get some free publicity?

- The general rule is that if a candidate is an incumbent, he or she would want fewer debates while if the candidate is a challenger, he or she would want more debates. That is simply because in most cases the incumbent will have better name recognition and does not want to give name ID to the challenger. There are some exceptions…If an incumbent is in trouble, he might want to have more debates; if a challenger has limited debating skills, he may not want to expose those oratorical weaknesses.

- Modern political "debates" are really not anything like the debates of Lincoln and Douglas. They tend more to be candidate forums where the candidates give commentaries on issues posed by a panel or from the audience. Before a debate or forum, a candidate should think through what questions he or she anticipates being asked and what the best response would be. If audience questions are permitted, a campaign should make sure that supporters are there who are prepared to ask "planted" questions that will either embarrass or challenge the opponent or make their candidate look like a genius.

- A wise candidate never makes claims that he or she knows to be false or which cannot be backed up with facts. Making a false or misleading statement in a debate can be a "killer" for the debate and fodder for a host of negative press and ads for the remainder of the campaign season. A candidate should be cautious about "winging it" if he or she is asked a question that the candidate does not understand or have an answer for. The candidate should ask for clarification if that is permitted. If that doesn't work a candidate should simply admit that he or she does not have an answer and offer to get back to the person that is asking the question.

> *It's important for a candidate to anticipate questions at a candidate debate or forum and think through appropriate responses.*

Chapter 11: Going After the Opponent

Without personally attacking an opponent, a candidate needs to attack the opponent's vote record or positions on the issues or show differences in qualifications. A candidate has to give voters a reason NOT to support the opponent. A candidate also has to continually put the opponent on the defensive.

Addressing an Opponent by Name

There are two schools of thought on a candidate using an opponent's name in advertising, news releases, at events and in doing interviews. One is that a campaign wants people to know who an opponent is and to associate the opponent's name with negative images. The second is that a campaign doesn't want to give an opponent more name recognition than that person would garner through his or her own campaign.

I advise candidates to consider the following: if an opponent is an incumbent or has campaign resources equal to or greater than yours, use your opponent's name. If your opponent is little known or has limited resources to get name recognition, don't use your opponent's name. Why give your opponent name recognition if he or she doesn't have it or can't get it?

If a candidate is going to use an opponent's name, he should strive to get voters to react negatively toward that name. If a candidate keeps hammering away at an opponent's record in office or what an opponent stands for, voters will start associating an opponent's name with matters that are distasteful to them. For example:

"State Representative Dave Doghouse continues to

vote against the people of this district. Doghouse voted for a tax increase that resulted in the closure of Sandman Industries"

Or

"I care about economic development, but apparently State Representative Dave Doghouse doesn't. In the last session of the legislature, Representative Doghouse voted against a bill to increase funding to train displaced workers..."

> **If an opponent is an incumbent with a bad record or has the resources to get name recognition, use that person's name in the campaign.**

Attacking Your Opponent Personally

Unless an opponent has committed a crime or was found guilty of moral or ethical lapses, it's always dangerous to attack an opponent personally. It's much safer and more effective to attack an opponent's vote record or his or her positions on the major issues. Instead of saying that an opponent is a lousy administrator, for example, it's better to point out <u>how</u> an opponent was a lousy administrator. Instead of saying that an opponent is a tool of special interests, it's better to question <u>why</u> an opponent got the support of some special interest.

If an opponent was found guilty of an ethical violation or criminal activity, that is fair game for a frontal attack by a candidate. If an opponent was accused or "rumored" to have engaged in some unflattering conduct, a candidate needs to use a great deal of discretion and caution. It is better for others and the media to question an opponent on those alleged shortfalls. Having a supporter writing a letter to the editor questioning an opponent's character can be more effective than if a candidate does it.

An opponent admitting having once tried marijuana or gotten thrown out of a bar while in college won't become an issue of importance in most campaigns. Let the media and the community "buzz" spread the word if an opponent has a clouded background. In many situations a candidate and his campaign need to step back and not nit-pick the opponent. Attacking an opponent on too many personal matters or matters that are inconsequential to a campaign can backfire.

Then there's the back-handed, good guy, slap-in-the-face approach that has been used since the start of the Republic:

> "I am not going to make an issue of my opponent's criminal record. I want to stick to the issues."

> **A candidate should avoid personal attacks on an opponent unless that opponent was found guilty of some ethical shortfall or criminal activity.**

Working Your Opponent's Areas of Strength

Many people advising campaigns tell candidates to work mainly in their areas of strength, not the areas of strength of their opponents. I totally disagree with that philosophy when it comes to competitive races. I was elected four times to my State Legislature in a district that normally voted 2-1 against the political party that I belonged to. Why?

While I didn't neglect those areas where my political party was more dominant, I spent about twice as much time working the areas of the district where my opponents would have had a more natural political following. During my first election I did respectable in the areas of strength of my opponent and mopped up the votes in the areas of my strength. By the time my fourth election rolled around I was doing equally well in areas where my opponent should have had a partisan advantage as I was in my party's strongholds.

It's a different story if a candidate is running for partisan office in an election district that is dominated by his or her political party. In such circumstances a candidate needs to "protect the base" and work hardest in his area of partisan strength. Even then a candidate should venture into the areas of the opponent's strength as an extra insurance policy.

Even in non-partisan elections, a candidate and his or her opponent will have pockets of strength and weakness in an election district. I know that I am repeating myself, but this is <u>important</u> to remember …For every vote that a candidate can switch from voting for his opponent to supporting him, he gains two votes! An opponent loses a vote and you gain a vote. Do the math.

> *In competitive races, a candidate should place priority on campaigning in the areas of an opponent's strength.*

Using Satire

The use of satire can be very effective but can be a disaster if used to denigrate an opponent in a hurtful or mean-spirited way. The best advice is for a candidate to carefully think through the use of satire before uttering it and to try to keep it somewhat funny or light-hearted. Some examples:

> "I can't blame my opponent for not knowing much about the county budget. After all, she has never been involved in making a county budget."

Or

> "John Typewriter can't possibly know the concerns of middle-class Americans. People seldom see him out of his mansion or limousine."

A candidate must be cautious with the use of satire.

Tackling Your Opponent While Being Nice

I once advised a candidate who was so false-heartedly nice to her opponent that by the time the campaign ended her opponent seemed afraid to be in her presence. One time she went up to her opponent and told him that he should have selected different colors for his campaign signs because the colors he selected were hard on the eyes. Another time she privately told him that his campaign brochure had too many words and showed him how to improve it. In several debate forums she openly stated that because she knew, liked and respected her opponent she couldn't believe how he had voted on several issues the way he did. She won by a landslide.

Showing respect to an opponent or being false-heartedly nice will drive an opponent crazy:

> *"I have a great deal of respect for Alderman Smith. Our kids go the same school together. That's why it's so disappointing that Alderman Smith..."*

Or

> *"I believe that Alderman Smith is a good person but so very wrong on the issues that are important to this community. For example, do you know that Alderman Smith voted against..."*

Or

> *"Alderman Smith is such a nice person. He's the type of guy you wouldn't mind sitting down and having a beer with. Unfortunately, Alderman Smith ..."*

> **Being polite and nice to an opponent can drive him crazy.**

Doing a Pledge Challenge

A good way for a candidate to back an opponent into a corner is to challenge him or her to sign a written pledge to support the popular side of a major issue. That is particularly appealing if a candidate knows that his or her opponent won't sign such a pledge.

In my years in politics I have seen pledge challenges effectively used to pin down candidates on tax, spending and social issues. A candidate making a pledge challenge generally gets some free publicity. The candidate being challenged either has to accept the pledge or explain to the public why he or she cannot support it.

Let me give you a real-life example... I once witnessed a candidate for local office issue a challenge to his incumbent opponent to oppose a highway by-pass around a community. The incumbent had a lot of support in the downtown business community that would lose business if the by-pass was constructed. However, the incumbent also had considerable campaign financial support from some powerful landowners where the new highway was proposed to go. The challenger sent the incumbent a written pledge to sign opposing the by-pass and sent out a news release to the same affect. The incumbent was caught between a rock and a hard place. The incumbent wouldn't sign the pledge and gave an instant issue to his challenger. The challenger hammered away at the incumbent for not signing the pledge during the remainder of the campaign. The challenger won by 20%.

When presented with a pledge challenge concerning a popular issue, the recipient has three choices:

a) Sign it and go along with the challenger on the issue. That will end the pledge issue matter but only after the challenging candidate has had some free press.

b) Refuse to sign it. That, of course, might be handing the challenging candidate an issue he or she can run with. By refusing to sign a pledge, a candidate being challenged should state why the pledge will go unsigned. That will give him or her chance to fire back on the challenger.

c) Sign, with qualifications. That will buy some time and possibly derail the challenge. It also gives the candidate being challenged an opportunity to send out his own news release announcing his decision and putting the other candidate on the defensive.

If the written pledge tactic is used: a) a news release should be sent out to garner some free publicity, b) the written pledge should be sent by certified mail so the recipient can't say he didn't receive it and c) a deadline date for responding should be included in a cover letter so that the opponent being challenged can't give the excuse that the matter is still under consideration.

> *Challenging an opponent to sign a written pledge can be an effective means of placing that individual in a corner.*

Mud Slinging Charge

A candidate is perfectly in his right to attack an opponent on the issues. It is called "mud-slinging" when a candidate maliciously attacks his or her opponent with misleading or false information. Saying that his or her opponent is engaging in "mud-slinging" can be very effective if, in fact, an opponent isn't being forthright.

There's a difference between "mud-slinging" and "negative campaigning." "Mud-slinging" is a malicious attack on an opponent that isn't intended to be totally truthful or attacks a candidate personally or is meant to be hurtful. "Negative campaigning," on the other hand, occurs when a candidate attacks his or her opponent's statements, positions or votes, but in a truthful manner.

The voting public has little stomach for raw "mud-slinging" while it will tolerate negative campaigning. In fact, there is a reason why most candidates engage in some negative campaigning...It works. A candidate and his or her supporters have to remember that in many cases people vote more <u>against</u> a candidate than <u>for</u> a candidate. In most campaigns there will be more negative attack ads than positive image ads simply because a winning candidate usually is the one who made the positions of an opposing candidate distasteful.

The way to make the charge that an opponent is "mud-slinging" is for a campaign to send out a news release based on a complaint to proper election officials. Election officials will usually respond that either a violation of fair election rules has occurred or that no law was violated. If a violation is determined to have occurred, the candidate filing the complaint will have a good issue on his side. If the latter is determined, the candidate filing the complaint can have a comeback that while no law was broken, the opponent should engage in positive campaigning by addressing the issues fairly and accurately.

A candidate should <u>never</u> file a frivolous complaint with election officials claiming "mud-slinging." I once had a candidate running against me who filed a complaint that was totally without basis. The head of the election oversight agency was so irritated with my opponent's complaint that he sent out his own news release blasting my opponent. That effectively ended my opponent's campaign against me.

The way for a candidate to avoid being charged with "mud-slinging" is

> *Properly orchestrated, filing an accurate complaint about "mud-slinging" can be effective.*

to always be honest in talking about what an opponent stands for. If an opponent's positions on the issues are unpopular with voters, by all means his challenger should attack those positions. Such attacks, however, must be truthful.

Filing an Elections Complaint

Election laws are often technical and strict. Meeting deadlines for making reports, properly using disclaimers, adhering to contribution and spending limits and the like are all spelled out in most election regulations.

I once saw a good candidate for a local sheriff's office get into a lot of trouble simply because his campaign forgot to have a disclaimer printed on yard sighs. His opponent badgered him for the rest of the campaign by filing a complaint with election officials and continually stating that the guilty party couldn't possibly enforce the law because he was caught breaking the law. In another instance I witnessed an incumbent finding out that a challenger had accepted more political donations than was allowable. The incumbent filed a complaint with election officials and spent the rest of the campaign questioning the ethics of his challenger.

There are three rules to follow if a candidate is going to make a complaint about an opponent's alleged violations of elections laws and regulations to election officials:

   a) Make sure that an alleged action of an opponent or his campaign actually has a basis for being a violation of election laws. Making a complaint that an opponent said something nasty about the way you part your hair might be mean, but it isn't illegal.

   b) Publicize the complaint with a news release or press conference. While a candidate might be filing a complaint for altruistic reasons of wanting to be a good citizen, he or she might as well pick up some free press and votes in the process.

c) Make sure that a complaint is grounded in accurate information. I once saw a good candidate lose an election after making a complaint to elections officials on hearsay rather than with substantiated proof that a violation of laws had occurred.

> *If it is confirmed that an opponent probably violated election laws, a candidate should file a complaint with election officials.*

Responding to the Opponent

I advise candidates not to respond to attacks if the opponent is telling the truth and to respond if the opponent isn't telling the truth.

Remember, a candidate doesn't want to give an opponent any opportunities to get name recognition and legitimacy. By responding to every little attack by an opponent a candidate will be doing just that. A candidate should only respond to attacks by an opponent if: a) he was attacked unfairly or untruthfully, b) he knows that the response being contemplated is accurate, and c) the response will give him or her an opportunity to reinforce a negative image of the opponent.

If a candidate does respond to an attack by an opponent, he or she should back up the response with documentation, vote records or statements that have been made previously. With proof in hand, a candidate should go after an opponent hard if an unfair or inaccurate claim has been made by the opponent. Again, a candidate should avoid attacking the character of his or her opponent. Rather, a candidate should go after the essence of the truthfulness or accuracy of an opponent.

DON'T say:
> "My opponent is a liar and clearly is misrepresenting my position. Mrs. Doorhinge knows full well that I voted against the tax increase. Mrs. Doorhinge wouldn't know the truth if it hit her in the face."

DO say:
> "The charge by Mrs. Doorhinge is unfortunate and inaccurate. It's not truthful. It's a lie. If she would have bothered to check the record, she would have found out that I voted against the tax increase. Mrs. Doorhinge should check the facts before making statements that are not true."

In the first example above the candidate is making a personal attack on his opponent by calling her a liar. In the second example the candidate is raising the specter that his opponent is not truthful or accurate without directly attacking his opponent as a person.

> *A candidate shouldn't respond to attacks that are truthful. If attacked unfairly, a candidate should respond by counter-attacking what an opponent said, but not the opponent.*

Opposition Research

In order to attack an opponent a candidate needs to do opposition research. If an opponent is an incumbent, he or she has a voting record that can be secured through minutes of committees or votes by a governing body. Has an opponent made public statements on issues that can be attacked? Has an opponent ever committed a crime?

A candidate <u>must give reasons</u> why he or she should be elected and not an opponent. Again, studies have shown that in many elections more people vote against a candidate than for a candidate. A campaign needs to research issues that a candidate can use as wedges between the voters and his or her opponent.

> *A campaign needs to research an opponent's positions on the issues that a candidate can attack.*

Anticipating Attacks

Just as a candidate will be attacking an opponent's positions on issues, he or she should expect an opponent to be doing the same. Have you ever cast a vote or made a statement that you later regretted? Have you ever had a business failure or gotten in trouble with the law? Have you ever taken a position that was right but difficult to explain in a short sound bite?

When being attacked, the natural inclination is to lash back. The trouble with that is that a candidate may come off as being too emotional or the response might not contain the well thought out points that he or she should be making. It is far better to be prepared with a response to anticipated attacks than to be caught off guard and make statements that will get you into more trouble than the original target of an opponent's attack.

A candidate should always be prepared to admit that he or she made a mistake if an opponent challenges a candidate on an issue or statement that the candidate really believes was wrong in hindsight. Admitting that an error was made makes a candidate look human and takes the issue in question off the table.

> *A wise candidate should anticipate how an opponent will attack him and what his response should be.*

Chapter 12: Getting Ready For the Next Campaign

If you follow much or all of the advice in the preceding eleven Chapters and its after Election Day, you hopefully are now an elected official. Congratulations! If you were elected, this chapter will help you in the next election. If you didn't get elected, go back to Chapter 1.

Thank Voters and Supporters

The next day after an election victory you need to thank the voters and especially those who actively supported your campaign. Voters and supporters want to know that they are appreciated. There are several things I would recommend that you do:

a) Send out a news release thanking the voters for their support and pledging to work hard to justify the faith they put in you. Also take the opportunity in the release to say a few kind words about your recent election opponent.

b) Have your campaign take out a few smaller ads in local newspapers or shoppers to thank voters for their support. In such ads just have your headshot picture and something simple like: "Thanks for your support for County Clerk. Sincerely, Mary Christmas."

c) Personally phone your major volunteers and contributors to thank them for their support. Make each supporter feel that you could not have been elected without their help. Tell them that *they* won the election, not you.

d) Sending a small gift to your main volunteers and

contributors is a nice gesture. There are companies that can personalize gifts with a local or state outline or seal or affix a flag. After one of my campaigns I sent out letter openers with the state seal at the top. After another I distributed American flag pins in a nice box. Such gifts don't need to be big or expensive. They just need to be a gesture of thanks.

> *Thanking voters and supporters needs to occur right after Election Day.*

Make the Rounds of the Media

Soon after the election, visit all media outlets covering your election district. The purpose of such visits can have many purposes:

a) Thank reporters, editors, and broadcast managers for covering your campaign. If you advertised with them, compliment them on the fine job they did with your ads.

b) Ask the media people you visit with if they have any questions. Oftentimes they will want to do "an exclusive" interview with you right on the spot. Take advantage of that opportunity for free publicity.

c) When visiting radio stations ask if they would like you to send in taped interviews or do phone interviews on a regular basis. Ask if they would like you to stop in for live talk show programs now and then.

d) When visiting the print media, see if they would like you to compose a weekly or monthly column for them. If so, send them a one column inch size professionally done heading with your picture, the name of your column, your name and the office you hold.

Visiting media outlets right after the election might be work, but it is worth it. Media folks will be impressed that you are ready to go to work for the people who just elected you.

> *Visit media outlets right after the election.*

Establish and Maintain Consistent Media Relations

Establishing and maintaining good media relations early on will pay dividends in getting your messages to citizens and your name constantly before the public. Isn't that what you tried to do during the campaign? Now it's free!

If the print media agrees to run a weekly or monthly column, make sure to keep the contents informational, not political. If you hold an executive position at the local or county level or are in the state legislature you will have plenty of topics to talk about. Never use your column for partisan rhetoric or to attack your adversaries. If you do that, readers will get turned off and your column will be yanked by the media. Rather, keep such a column as a forum to discuss the pros and cons of an issue or to inform citizens about programs or policies.

Take advantage of the opportunity to send news releases to media outlets covering your election district. Unlike during a campaign, media outlets are not as fussy about requiring that news releases of sitting officeholders be based on a speech before a group. Delivering a speech and then sending out a news release based on that appearance, however, adds credibility to the release. If you are speaking before a group, try to have a friend or supporter take a picture of you speaking to go along with the news release for the print media.

The electronic media will sometimes agree to take and use taped interviews or do interviews over the phone. That is particularly useful if you hold a state legislative seat and the statehouse is 300 miles from a local radio station. If possible, do such commentaries on a regular basis.

Get in the habit of calling TV and radio stations to see if they have any questions or to arrange a time for you to stop in for an interview. Most TV and radio stations will want to interview you and may use your comments during newscasts throughout the day.

Regularly participating in radio talk shows or call-in programs is a good way to communicate with the electorate. When I was a state legislator, I tried to make it to such programs at each station 2-3 times per year. As you should have done during the campaign, have supporters call in "planted" questions during call-in programs.

If you ran a small campaign or had limited financial resources and didn't advertise on TV, don't let that stop you from making contact with TV personnel. Most TV stations have local reporters who will relish the opportunity to interview you for the local news.

The important things for a public official in managing media relations are: a) be accurate, b) be informative and c) be consistent. Regular contacts with media people with accurate, informative commentaries will be appreciated by media outlets and their audiences or subscribers.

> *Establishing and maintaining consistent media relations is important.*

Use Social Media and a Web Page

Now that you are an incumbent officeholder, people will check out your web page or make posts in social media platforms to be informed and engaged in public affairs. Use these means of communication to talk about issues you are working on, provide information of general interest to the public and invite readers to express their views. Make sure to provide your contact information and places where people can post comments or ask questions. Update your web and social media pages regularly and respond to inquiries from citizens just as you would if you received letters or emails from them.

Attend Community Events

You thought that going to fairs, community festivals, and church picnics were over with at the end of the campaign and your election? Nope. Now you are an elected official. You might not be campaigning per se but you have a duty to be where your people are. You need to be "out and about" listening to their concerns. That's important as a "public servant" and it is also good long-term politics.

The good thing about attending local community events after you are elected is that it's more relaxing and less "political". You aren't trying to gain votes and you aren't being followed by a political opponent. You are simply mingling with the people and they will appreciate that. You will find that going around a table at a neighborhood or church picnic and shaking hands is a lot easier when you are an elected official and not just a candidate who is looking for votes.

While I am not a fan of booths at community events during campaigns because you miss too many people, having a booth at a community fair or festival can be effective during non-campaign periods. People might not seek you out at a booth during a campaign, but they might want to stop by and talk to you now that you are an elected official. If you do have a booth at a local event, make sure that your booth has your name and office on a prominent sign and that the booth is decorated in a patriotic theme.

Weather walking around a community event or being stationary in a booth; it's a good idea to have a small handout to give to attendees. Again, a sports schedule or a calendar on a business card sized handout works well. On the reverse side have your picture, name and office. Leave off the "elect" and the disclaimer you used during the campaign because you are not technically campaigning (leave on the disclaimer if your campaign committee is paying for the handout). Is there a printing allotment for your office that you can use for the printing costs of the handout?

> **Attend community events to listen to the concerns of people.**

Go to Parades and Public Events

Get in a convertible, on a hay wagon or on the back of a truck and attend community parades. It's a great way to be seen by hundreds or thousands of your constituents with very little effort.

A few parade suggestions for elected officials: a) have your family with you if possible, b) dress up your parade entry in patriotic colors and flags, c) be sure your name and the office you hold is on a prominent sign on both sides of your entry (no "elect" and no disclaimer on your sign unless your campaign committee paid for it), and d) simply waive and say "hi" to people you pass by in the parade route. If you feel comfortable with it, walk along the parade route and shake hands or pass out some sort of handout.

Is there an open house for a new business in town or a bridge dedication? How about a groundbreaking for a new school? Is an important person coming to town to give a speech? How about the annual community Christmas concert or Memorial Day ceremony? For some of these events the only thing you need to do is show up, maybe shake a few hands and smile. No handouts to pass out. No speeches to make.

If you are invited to give a talk at a public event, continue to remember K.I.S.S. Keep it short, informative and inspirational.

At ceremonies, dedications, open houses and other similar public events a local newspaper reporter and photographer will likely show up. There's a little trick you should use if there is a group photo at such an event. Unless it is required that you stand in the center for a photo or you are directed to be in a specific spot, position yourself on the far-LEFT side (camera's view) of the group being photographed. Why? When the caption under the photo appears in the newspaper which name will be read first?

> *Participation in parades and public events is a good way to be seen by voters.*

Going Door-To-Door

Just as going door-to-door was an effective tool in getting you elected, it can be an effective tool in bonding you and your constituency. People expect to see candidates going door-to-door during campaign time. They will be shocked to see their local alderman, county clerk or state legislator at their door between elections. I used to enjoy going door-to-door between elections. It gave me an opportunity to meet the citizens that I was serving and learn of their concerns. It was also good exercise and smart politics.

As an elected official, the door-to-door routine is this: a) briefly introduce yourself, b) say that you are in the neighborhood to hear the concerns of citizens, c) ask if they have any concerns and d) leave them with a business card that they can stick in their wallet or purse. The business card is legitimate public business and should be paid out of your official printing allotment if you have one. If the handout is being paid for by your campaign committee you must have a disclaimer on it in most jurisdictions.

I had a special doorknob hanger made for going door-to-door between elections. The top portion was a message from me indicating that I was in the neighborhood to hear from citizens. The top portion message also indicated that recipients should keep the business card at the bottom of the doorknob hanger should they want to contact me. The bottom portion business card had a perforation separating it from the rest of the hanger. When I ran into people at home, I gave them only the business card that I had already separated from the hanger. When people were not home, I simply left the hanger on the doorknob and moved to the next house.

I found that people were usually startled that I was at their door as a sitting State Senator. Very few people expressed opinions or had questions. I kept a notebook and pen with me to write things down when they did have something to say or wanted me to look up something for them.

After my first election I knew I needed to shore up support where an opposing candidate in the future would have a natural base of support. Between my first and second elections I hit every neighborhood I could where my original vote total was less than 50%. I attribute my second election largely on the fact that I took the time to visit those neighborhoods before the second campaign season started.

> *Going door-to-door between elections is good public service and smart politics.*

Keeping in Communication with Individuals

Elected officials are bound to get a fair amount of mail, emails, Faxes, messages on social media pages and phone calls from their constituents. It's important that those communications be answered promptly and accurately. If some subject of a citizen inquiry needs research, at least indicate to the citizen that you are working on it and will get back to that person as soon as you can. Consider contacting your constituent with an update report if getting an answer to their inquiry is going to take more time than expected.

People want to know that an elected official read their concerns and that the office holder is personally getting back to them. The only time I used a "form letter" communication by mail or electronically was when I received form letters. For example, if I received 100 post cards from the members of some special interest group with the same message but different signatures and addresses, I replied with 100 form letters back.

People usually like it when their picture is in the paper or there is a favorable article about what they are doing or some accomplishment they achieved. I had some congratulatory cards made up that I just needed to sign. In it I inserted a clipping about the recipient from their local newspaper. Most people were impressed that I noticed an article or photo about them. Kick the winning field goal in an important game, send a card. Get engaged, send a card. Open a new business, send a card. It makes the recipients feel good and they will remember you on Election Day.

Many elected officials are given an office mailing and printing account to communicate with constituents. When

I served in the Wisconsin Senate, each legislator was allowed to do a district-wide mailing once every two years which was charged to his or her office account. That was a great way of getting positions on issues out and accomplishments given notice. I alternated my district-wide mailings between a legislative report and an opinion survey. I was always surprised by the number of surveys that were actually filled out and returned. Such surveys were good opinion indicators to me and also served the purpose of people knowing that I cared about their concerns.

Even if an elected official cannot personally afford to send out a mailing or doesn't have an office expense allotment, printing and distributing a periodic flyer or newsletter is smart. Even a short, inexpensive newsletter printed on both sides of a sheet of paper can serve the purpose. It would only take a few volunteers and an hour or two to hand deliver such a piece to each home in a neighborhood.

> *Good communication is good government and good politics.*

Disarm the Enemy

Are there individuals or groups that supported your opponent in the last election that you can approach?

Two days after my first election to the Wisconsin State Senate I drove 60 miles to attend a meeting of an organization that strongly supported my recently defeated opponent. To say the least, the group members almost had a communal heart attack when I showed up at the meeting. When called upon to say a few words I said that I knew they had strongly opposed me in the election but that I hoped we could work together for the betterment of the region. The president of the organization called me the next day to say how impressed and pleased he was that I attended the meeting. I never did get the endorsement of that group in subsequent elections, but the organization didn't vigorously oppose me in campaigns either.

I always made a point of trying to touch base with the supporters of my opponents that appeared on campaign contribution reports after each election. I either met them in person or phoned them and said that I knew they supported my opponent, but that I hoped to be able to work to gain their trust. Sure, some of them were rude, but the vast majority appreciated the gesture and became less vociferous supporters of my opponents in subsequent elections. Many of them actually became good political supporters of mine.

> *You should approach individuals and organizations that opposed you; show them that you care.*

Hold Office Hours

As a public official, one of the things that voters in future elections will remember is the fact that you made efforts to listen to their problems, concerns and opinions.

I always made it a point to hold open office hours so people could come in and meet with me in person. While representing an eight-county legislative district, I made a habit of spending a day in each county on a regular basis holding office hours. I would schedule 5-6 stops in a county at different locations, usually at a school or in local government building. I scheduled office hours to last about 45 minutes with 15 minutes in each hour left to drive to the next location. Whenever possible, I tried to schedule media visits and attend a meeting of a local club or organization while in each county.

The office hours regiment gave me several opportunities to garner media attention: a) a news release was sent out before a county tour announcing that I would be in county, b) interviews with the local media while on tour and c) a news release from the speaking event I attended while in the county.

Unless a group came into an office hour location with the same thing they wanted to talk to me about, I always offered to keep conversations with individual attendees private if anyone wished. Oftentimes people had personal problems that needed attention and did not want to share their issues with others in the room.

Sometimes I had dozens of people attending an office hour. There were other times, however, when I shivered alone in a rural town hall in the middle of January with no visitors. No matter! Voters at election time knew that I had paid visits to their community and that I was open to listening to their concerns.

When I became a city Mayor, I still held office hours, but at one location, the City Hall. People were welcome to come in and talk with me during one hour each week that was set aside for that purpose. Reminders that I had such open office hours were periodically announced in the local media.

I contend that holding office hours and making yourself available to citizens makes you a better public official. It also is good politics if you intend to run for re-election.

> *Hold office hours on a regular basis to meet with the people.*

Thanks for reading. I hope that these words of advice have been helpful! Just remember that good government is also good politics.

Made in the USA
Middletown, DE
28 November 2020